Science Knowledge and the Environment

A Guide for Students and Teachers in Primary Education

Michael Littledyke, Keith Ross and Liz Lakin

David Fulton Publishers
London

David Fulton Publishers Ltd
Ormond House 26–27 Boswell Street, London WC1N 3JD

First published in Great Britain by David Fulton Publishers 2000

British Library Cataloguing in Publication Data

A catalogue record for this book is available from the British Library

ISBN 1–85346–625–5

Typeset by Textype Typesetters, Cambridge
Printed in Great Britain by The Cromwell Press Ltd, Trowbridge, Wilts.

Contents

Acknowledgements

We would like to thank Keith Brooke, Dick Hanson and Craig Pepperell, as members of the Learning Support Unit, and George Burch, who have been centrally involved in the development of course study guides and CD ROMs used for science education courses for initial teacher education at Cheltenham and Gloucester College of Higher Education. This work has contributed significantly to the development of the content of this book.

Introduction

Michael Littledyke

The challenge

The famous and entrancing image of 'Spaceship Earth' obtained by the first lunar expedition as the explorers looked back to their home has done much to enhance our awareness of the vital importance of conserving our planet as the provider of the conditions for existence for humans and all other known forms of life. This beautiful picture portrays, in a powerfully symbolic yet tangible way, a finite world with limited resources and with a capacity for terminal damage from human activity. The major challenge with which we are now faced as a species is how to act on the message which this image presents so that we can develop a sustainable relationship with the Earth.

The timing of this book is auspicious in that we can look backwards at the twentieth century as the period of maximum environmental impact by humans in their history, while looking forward to a new era of potential improvement by drawing on and learning from this experience. As we enter the new millennium it has become clear that issues concerned with environmental relations present the most challenging and significant areas for choices and action both politically and personally. This book's purpose, therefore, is to consider how to address education for children to become informed and concerned adults who will be able to understand critically the implications of these choices and act wisely in the wider interests of society and the planet as a whole. Such education must start in the primary school, as this is a centrally important arena where the foundations for the understandings and values of future adults are prepared. In acknowledgement of this, this book is directed towards primary teachers and student teachers to provide support for their own understanding of the issues and a rationale for teaching children about the environment with the aim of developing in them informed views and responsible actions as adults of the future. We hope also that it may have a wider appeal both to teachers and the public in general.

Environmental reason and environmental concern

Environmental concern, encompassing values and attitudes towards the environment, and environmental reason, including scientific understanding of environmental issues, must be developed together to achieve balanced views. This book focuses on how science can be used to develop both of these features. This acknowledges science as a powerful tool for reason which can inform and give credibility to important concerns about the environment. Informed concern is necessary to lead to appropriate action which is in the interests of the environment and consequently beneficial to people who are sustained by it. Enlightened self-interest is a useful concept here. When people understand that all of life is interrelated and interdependent in a very real way, and that their existence depends on maintaining this, appropriate environmental action becomes an imperative rather than a choice. If we damage the systems that support us we inevitably damage ourselves, our children and their offspring, as well as other living things. The teacher's challenge is to help children become aware of this so that their actions as adults will improve their own lives and those of future generations.

This book supports this process by exploring how features of the environment function, which is the main project of science, while making explicit how human actions and choices can have particular impact. The central approach, therefore, is to show how scientific understanding is essential to understanding conse-quences of action as chains, sequences and complex interactions of linked systems. This will be demonstrated through looking at the main scientific ideas and processes which are embodied in the National Curriculum (DfE 1995) and in the standards for primary science for initial teacher education (DfEE 1998), while showing how the ideas are essential in developing understanding of important features of the environment and key environmental issues. In this way the title *Science Knowledge and the Environment* reflects the approach in the book which uses scientific understanding as an essential tool to inform and justify environmental concern and appropriate environmental action.

National Curriculum science and environmental education

Science, as a core National Curriculum subject, has achieved high status in the primary curriculum in recent years and the teaching of science has undoubtedly improved in quantity and quality. However, education has been subject to conflicting pressures from the policies of central government which prioritise the raising of standards with emphasis on knowledge and skills, while aspects of affective education, including beliefs, values and attitudes receive less attention (Gayford and Dillon 1995). While many teachers value the importance of environmental education, which has been identified as a cross-curricular theme in the National Curriculum (NCC 1990a), they are often unable to give it the attention which they consider it deserves because of pressure to cover the content of National Curriculum subjects, particularly the core subjects (Littledyke 1994a, 1997b). Also, there have been attempts to design initial teacher education courses which include environmental education as a component linked with science (e.g. Papadimitriou 1996; Jiménez *et al.* 1996) or as a discrete element (Fien 1995), but pressure to address subject content in more traditional ways can militate against the development of environmental education. This is a highly significant problem given the need for effective environmental education in a world of increasing environmental degradation. In an attempt to counter this worrying trend the rationale provided here has two important aims:

- to enable teachers to use 'the environment' as a meaningful and important context for learning science;
- to use the science curriculum to inform environmental education.

This will enable teachers to work within the framework of the National Curriculum (as they must by virtue of the legislation which enshrines it) whilst preparing their children for the environmental choices and challenges which await them in the future.

The term environment embraces all the conditions affecting the life of living organisms. In ecology (which is the study of living things, their surroundings and how they interact with each other and the surroundings) this refers to the physical (or abiotic) environment, and the living (or biotic) environment. This wide definition of environment provides an opportunity to look at the whole of the science National Curriculum as a potential context for environmental education. The content of the science National Curriculum, therefore, directly informs children's understanding of their environment. It is only a short step to linking this with approaches towards looking at ways of maintaining and improving the quality of the environment – the basis of environmental education.

Environmental education has commonly been defined as education:

- *about* the environment (including understanding of environmental matters);
- *in* and *through* the environment (including direct experience of studying and working in the environment); and
- *for* the environment (as concerned with values and attitudes appropriate to environmental protection) (NCC 1990a).

All these approaches have relevance to science education and we will demonstrate here how this may be achieved. In the spirit of its title this book will primarily emphasise the first point, where science knowledge is used to inform issues *about* the environment, while strategies for teaching will inevitably lead into learning *in* and *through* the environment in a range of contexts which will be illustrated *through* a number of case studies. Understanding of the issues (*about*) and experience of a range of contexts for learning (*in* and *through*) will enhance children's motivation for action to benefit the environment (*for*). It is hoped that this informed motivation will carry through into adulthood and contribute to the development of environmentally responsible citizens.

Children's learning in these areas, as in other areas of the curriculum, is dependent on the pedagogical skill and understanding of the teacher. Therefore, this book is designed to support teachers' and student teachers' needs for professional development which will enhance their teaching of science and environmental education. The factors influencing professional development in teaching science and the environment are shown in Figure 1. Teachers' understanding of science and the environment, how children learn, and approaches to teaching are influenced by each other. To be an effective teacher and enhance children's understanding of the environment all three areas need to be developed. The book addresses features of all these areas of teachers' learning to develop expertise in teaching science for environmental understanding, though the primary focus is on personal understanding to inform the other elements. To address all three elements extensively is beyond the scope of this book.

Summary of the content of the chapters

Chapters one to three examine issues of children's learning in science, the relationships between science and the environment and the implications for teaching.

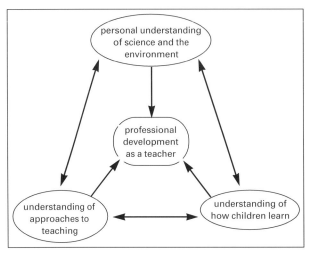

Figure 1: The factors influencing professional development of teaching of primary science and the environment

These chapters provide important perspectives to inform appropriate approaches to teaching. Chapter one focuses on children's development of scientific concepts and how this can support their understanding of the environment. These ideas lie at the heart of the book; meaningful understanding of important concepts in science will directly inform children's understanding of the environment and provide powerful reasons for action to protect the environment. This is as true for teachers as it is for children; when teachers have a sound understanding of the concepts they will be able to plan and teach science in a way which will support environmental education. Chapters two and three explore the effects of science on attitudes to the environment by highlighting some key features in thedevelopment of science and its environmental impact, as well as tracing developments in environmentalist views to support the environment. The ideas presented in these two chapters show that science has had profound influence on Western thought and approaches to technology. The implications of this for approaches to science and education for environmental understanding are discussed.

Chapters four to nine present essential science concepts and processes which provide important background to inform teachers' and student teachers' understanding of important environmental issues. Implications for teaching are considered for each area and some examples of activities and projects are shown as illustrative case studies. Emphasis is placed on the 'big ideas' in science and how these inform understanding of consequences of actions which impact on the environment. These ideas are presented in a way which will support teachers' understanding of the issues, but some guidance is given to show how they can also be adapted at a suitable level for children's understanding.

Much of the content of the book is drawn extensively from the authors' research into science and environmental education, including materials which have been developed for science courses for students at Cheltenham and Gloucester College of Higher Education. This includes two CD-ROMs, *The Science of Environmental Issues* and *The Science of Everyday Life*, course handbooks and research reports and papers in educational journals presenting research into teachers' practice and children's learning in science and environmental education (Littledyke 1996, 1997a, 1997b; Littledyke *et al.* 1997; Ross and Lakin 1996, 1998).

Chapter 1

Constructing a scientific understanding of our environment

Keith Ross

The purpose of an education in science

Each age sees the world differently, but the images initiated by Rachel Carson (1962) in the 60s and emphasised by Spaceship Earth with which we began this book, must provide the imperative and purpose behind an education in science for the 21st century.

While many have an emotional ('no GM food!') response to environmental protection, an emotional imperative alone cannot and should not be our reason for protecting the environment. There are impelling scientific reasons underpinning and qualifying these calls for action and they must be understood by a majority of us to achieve the task of moving the human race away from environmental decay and towards sustainable development.

A few examples are needed to make this point clear.

- Someone who drives a car five miles especially to put their bottles in a bottle bank may find that the exhaust fumes generated do more environmental harm than dumping the bottles on the tip (moral – recycle materials when the journey is going to be made anyway).
- Someone defacing GM crop trials to prevent possible genetic contamination may find that herbicide and pesticide used with conventional (non-organic) agriculture does even more damage (moral – think global, act locally – though it is difficult to justify a company selling GM seeds which can only be used beneficially if you buy their own make of herbicide).
- Someone campaigning against storage of nuclear waste may find that fossil fuel powerstations do more environmental damage, and use up more non-replenishable reserves – just as the rocks in which the waste is being stored are non-replenishable since they too are not able to be used by future generations. (Moral – judge issues on scientific, rather than emotional grounds).

Some argue that science is too difficult for most of us to understand, so we have to rely on 'experts'. We have no choice but to build up emotional responses – the science is inaccessible. We disagree. The science is hard, but we argue in this book that humans can obtain a sufficient scientific understanding to make judgements on what the 'experts' say. An ignorant population will have a majority who don't care, and a minority whose only weapon is emotion – carefully ignored by the majority.

Giving school science an everyday context

So where is this scientific understanding going to come from? School science, especially at secondary level, seems to be too academic and remote for the majority. It becomes an end in itself – why, for example, do we make hot water in school laboratories using a Bunsen Burner? An unthinking answer might be 'Because Bunsens have always been used, they are fun, and an essential part of school science.' The danger is that school science becomes built up as a knowledge system remote from real life and real issues. Many excellent attempts have been made to bring school science into the lives of the pupils, and primary science has usually shown the way.

An early attempt at doing this, *Brenda and Friends* (West 1984; Ross 1998), was published several years before the first science National Curriculum. It was an attempt to sketch out a 'minimum entitlement' for pupils who follow a course in science during the compulsory years at school. The discussion paper, part of the Secondary Science Curriculum Review, set out ways that an education in science could increase educational opportunity. It described the content of such a programme, with Brenda and each of her friends illustrating how the science they had experienced at school, from reception to 16+, had changed and developed the way they thought about their world. How wonderful if the new National Curriculum orders (published in 2000) and the syllabuses and examinations of the GCSE boards were written in this form rather than in academic topics, with the teachers left to try to make them real.

Tackling misconceptions

Our task of giving the next generation an understanding of how their environment works would only be half done, even when we teach science through environmental issues. An equally big problem lies with misconceptions which develop as we experience our environment and try to make sense of it. Children come to school with naive ideas already forming. These are often contradicted by our present scientific understanding. The words the children use for these ideas are often inappropriate. In this respect, their *thinking* can often be *conceptually* acceptable, though they may be using words inappropriately and will need to develop accepted labels to these ideas. Can you pick out the *grains of truth* in what the children (and adults!) are saying in the examples that follow, but also point out the misconceptions? The references are to the chapters in this book where these grains of truth are discussed.

1. Burning destroys things (Chapter 5 and used as a case study here).
2. Wax is fireproof (Chapter 5).
3. Water in a drying puddle disappears (Chapter 5).
4. Hot air rises (Chapter 5).
5. Energy is used up (Chapter 6).
6. Petrol is turned into energy in the car (Chapter 6).
7. Plants feed on soil through their roots (Chapter 8).
8. Apple trees make apples for us to eat (Chapter 8).
9. Air keeps us alive (Chapters 5 and 9).
10. Food is turned into energy in our body (Chapters 6 and 9).

These are all naive ideas which are based on direct experience, and used by us in our everyday lives but they all lead to misunderstandings of the scientific ideas which lie behind them. Science education for many learners leaves many of these misconceptions intact. The chapters that follow document many which underpin an understanding of the environment. We examine number 1, *Burning destroys things*, here, to provide a framework for an education in science that might enable more of us to understand how the environment works.

The conservation of atoms

Burning does destroy things, like wood, although it doesn't destroy the atoms which make up the wood. However, when our teachers say that atoms are the particles which make up wood, the pupils imagine that the atoms are little bits of wood and that they burn up just like the wood itself. As teachers we need to understand that children's ideas which are built up through everyday experiences tend to be descriptive, and that our scientific ideas are often counter-intuitive. The wood burns but the atoms are unchanged – how can that be? This chapter looks at the process of conceptual change and how children construct meaning for themselves. This needs to be understood if teachers are to challenge the firmly held but often mistaken ideas held by children which otherwise persist into adulthood. First we continue with our example.

An idea vital for an understanding of how the planet works is the concept of the atom. Research (reported below) has suggested that about half of those training to be primary teachers and who have gained a grade C at GCSE science think that atoms can behave like bulk matter during change – melting, burning and boiling just as the substances themselves do.

Does it matter that most people don't understand about atoms? Materials can be destroyed – they disappear. You throw materials away, down the drain, on the tip or into the air, and they're gone. The impression is that you buy something in the shops, use it and throw it away – that's how the world *seems* to work. But if this is the case, why are environmentalists going on about greenhouse gases, insecticide residues, and all this recycling of cans and paper?

It is a worrying but striking assertion that children (and adults) have these strongly held alternative but naive ideas, as in our atoms example, and this assertion needs to be justified before we develop our constructivist approach to learning – an attempt to tackle these firmly held beliefs.

Evidence for lack of conservation of atoms

The Science of Environmental Issues is a core science module for the 3-year primary BEd degree at the Cheltenham and Gloucester College of Higher Education. It is supported by two principles: a constructivist approach to learning to identify and tackle students' alternative ideas in science; and an environmental theme, to provide a purposeful context for their study. The module occupies a tenth of every primary trainee teacher's year one programme and is organised into 6 units covering much of the Science National Curriculum (DfE 1995):

- Matter (pollution, resource management and waste)
- Genetics (genetic engineering)
- Atmosphere (greenhouse effect, ozone depletion and acid rain)
- Biodiversity (habitat loss and evolution)
- Energy (the fuel crisis)
- Radioactivity (concerns about the nuclear industry).

Students attend a lead lecture in each unit and then study with help of a work-book, a CD-Rom (Ross and Lakin 1996, 1998) and additional tutor-led workshops.

We have been using learning logs and concept mapping as a learning and assessment tool for some years to allow students to reflect on their understandings and to get immediate feedback from their assignments. Figure 1.1 contains quotations from a few of these logs. We also administer by computer a pre-module objective test to help students select those units they would be most able to cope with by self-study. The test is also used at the end of the module to assess progress. Our understanding of the scientific ideas held by these teachers in training comes from these data. The data refer to a cohort of 63 students mentioned above.

Those whose scientific understanding of the permanence of atoms was weak on arrival were identified from their learning logs. The comment in Figure 1.1 '*I had never realised that these atoms could not be destroyed*' and that they remain after the material had been destroyed was typical of 30 of the students who all admitted to thinking, at the start of the module, that atoms could be destroyed during chemical changes such as burning or digestion.

Evidence for conceptual change was also obtained by looking at the change to responses to individual questions from the pre- to the post-test. The question below is one of seven questions that tested for an understanding of the conservation of atoms:

> Consider the *material* (stuff, matter, atoms . . .) in our food that enters our blood and which we have *used as a fuel*. Which of the following describes how this *material* leaves our body? (Choose true, false or don't know for each alternative)

(a) The atoms are all used up and only energy is left.
    Chosen by 23 (37 per cent) as true at start and by just one at end
(b) It comes out as faeces.
(c) We breathe a lot of it out as carbon dioxide and water vapour.
(d) It comes out as energy, e.g. movement and heat.

All those making learning log comments similar to that shown in Figure 1.1 also showed a marked improvement in their test scores in these seven 'conservation' questions. In this way the learning logs provided validation for using the test scores as evidence of conceptual change. These results have been replicated for six successive cohorts over three years.

The data from the tests and learning logs provide us with a number of other examples where students have retained a naive view of the way the environment works, despite their best attempts to make sense of their GCSE science. As we have already said, chapters 4–9 identify some of these misconceptions and attempt to explain why they are so persistent.

We now return to our theme – a constructivist approach to teaching that takes account of these naive ideas.

'I had never realised that these atoms could not be destroyed, and that they remain after the material had been destroyed. The idea that burning is a constructive process [adding oxygen atoms] was also new to me, but became obvious after the explanations.'

'I found the principles of burning very enlightening. The constructive process of oxygen forming oxides and increasing weight now seems very obvious.'

'I gradually came to realise how much of a part 'atoms' do play in matter. I have always assumed that as materials go though the process of change, the atoms from which they are made up, change too. However, this unit helped me to understand that atoms are indestructible and I can look at any substance now and judge that regardless of what change it goes through, atoms will remain the same.'

Figure 1.1 Learning log comments made by trainee teachers – all of whom left school with a Grade C or better in double award science at GCSE

Constructivist approaches to learning

Changing people's ideas about how the planet, its life and life support systems work and function is not straightforward – ideas are difficult to change. Beliefs, once held, become entrenched. This section looks at conceptual change, and the importance of challenging naive ideas at a young age, before they become embedded and unquestioned.

These 'alternative' conceptions have been thoroughly researched in science (Driver *et al.* 1994; SPACE 1989–92). Our own research, described above, has only served to reinforce the message.

Ausubel (1968) put forward three conditions that have to be fulfilled if learners are to understand, with meaning, the ideas and concepts they are presented with by their teachers:

1. The material must be understood by the teacher/presenter.
2. The learner must have appropriate knowledge and experiences onto which the new ideas can build, and the teacher needs to find these out.
3. The learners must want to learn – they need a reason to justify putting in an effort to think.

We can add to these one from Bruner (1966):

4. The learner needs to make use of their new knowledge, to keep it active and relevant.

Since then teaching approaches have been trialled to give learners the maximum opportunity to construct their own meaning. Many have been involved in this constructivist movement, but the work of the late Rosalind Driver in Leeds is perhaps the most inspiring.

Driver (1985), commenting on Ausubel's ideas, highlights the need to consider the child's preconceptions observing that:

- they are amazingly tenacious and resistant to change;
- the unlearning of preconceptions might well prove to be the most determinative single factor in the acquisition and retention of subject matter knowledge.

She identifies four pointers for classroom practice:

- Curriculum development needs to pay attention to the structure of thought of the child. There is a need for a shift from logical processes (Piaget) to conceptual ideas.
- Teaching programmes need to be structured to be more in keeping with the developmental paths in understanding more important ideas. The logical order of teaching a topic may not correspond to the psychological order of learning. (She expresses caution about structured learning programmes.)
- We need activities which challenge alternative interpretations as well as those which confirm accepted ones.
- We must allow children time to think through implications of their observations and measurements made in science lessons. Teacher explanations do not always spring clearly from the data.

A constructivist approach for conservation of matter

Drawing on the above, we now present a model for a *constructivist* approach to teaching and learning. It will be illustrated by our conservation of atoms theme (adapted from Driver and Bell 1986, see also Littledyke and Huxford 1998 and Ollerenshaw and Ritchie 1993).

Although the following sequence is appropriate for KS3 it can be simplified for use in the primary school. It is used here for two purposes:

1. It tackles a concept which research suggests is only understood by half those entering primary teacher training, but which all teachers must understand if they are to fulfil Ausubel's first condition for meaningful learning: unless teachers understand the fate of substances thrown away, how can they begin to embed this understanding into their teaching, and understand the stages through which children must proceed to achieve this understanding?
2. It illustrates a constructivist approach to learning.

Burning is a constructive process

Orientation or impact
Arousing children's interest and curiosity.

Show the class some logs of firewood, and a shovelful of ashes. This gives the *impact* and *context* for the learning.

Elicitation
Helping children find out and clarify what they think.

Ask the pupils to think what the wood is made from – where did all that matter come from as the tree grew – and where does it all go when the log is burnt?

Finding out individual ideas from each child in a class of 30 may seem an impossible task. Most teachers wait for hands to go up when they ask a question requiring an oral answer. But if you ask the class: 'Whisper to each other where you think the materials come from (water, soil, air, sun . . .)', each pupil will whisper their idea to their neighbour, allowing them to think it out for themselves and to rehearse a verbal response without making a fool or exhibition of themselves. Those without an answer hear one from their neighbour.

You can now collect a few ideas in whole-class mode. Pupils who are not asked are still able to think to themselves 'yes – that's what I said', or 'I didn't think that'). You now ask if anyone else thought that way, or if there are any other ideas and can put it to the vote, thus *eliciting* the ideas of each of your pupils.

The Channel 4 (1993) television programme 'Simple Minds' tried this elicitation on MIT graduates in the USA, with horrifying results – the idea that a tree was made largely from carbon obtained from the air was unacceptable to many of them.

Also *elicit* their ideas about the process of burning 'Whisper to each other what you think happens to the stuff the wood is made of when it is burnt'. You can show the ashes, or better actually burn a twig in front of them, so some can see the fumes and smoke being produced.

Intervention
Providing the learners with experiences, ideas, stories which will enable them to make better sense of the phenomenon and to challenge, modify or confirm their beliefs.

All sorts of experiences may be needed before pupils are ready for the full picture at KS3 involving the gas carbon dioxide. At KS2 they will need experience that gases are material substances – perhaps by weighing a football before and after pumping it hard. They can see that burning wood, or a candle, goes out if air is excluded, and they can see condensation (of water) as a product of burning. By placing that jar over a lighted candle they can see that the fumes from burning are not the same as fresh air (the candle won't stay alight in them). For further discussion and ideas see Chapter 5, Matter and Life.

Re-interpretation or restructuring
Helping children clarify what they think and encouraging them to test their ideas and extend, develop or replace them following the intervention (or teaching) phase.

With new ideas moving in along side the old, or even replacing some of them (wood is destroyed, but its atoms are not), children need time to build or reinterpret these ideas into their own cognitive structure. They first need to be able to do this verbally, by explaining the ideas to each other. This can be done with a quick 'tell each other' session. Any texts that they read need to be reflected on using DARTs (see Figure 1.2). They then need to take time to write it in their own words. Sutton (1992) develops the idea of 'word work' to describe these opportunities for pupils to reflect on scientific ideas. He develops the idea of audience (Barnes 1976). Pupils writing for their teacher as an 'examiner who knows the right answer' may play the game of writing what they think the teacher wants to read (Driver 1975). The chance to write for a more friendly audience, where the pupil knows more than their reader, gives the writer more freedom and confidence. They are more likely to write what they believe. (See Figure 1.3 – creative writing.) This may uncover misconceptions that the child still has, so their efforts need to be read positively but carefully.

Evaluation and use
Helping children to relate what they have learned to their everyday lives.

It is worrying when a trainee teacher says 'I can't remember that – I last did chemistry four years ago.' Ideas that are not useful and used in your everyday life soon become forgotten. The sort of science we want children to understand relates directly to understanding their lifestyle and their environment. Shortly after the wood lesson above we need to reactivate the pupils' awareness, and get them to think about plant growth and burning rubbish. At KS3 we can ask them to explain why burning fossil fuels releases carbon dioxide to the atmosphere, and why cutting down forests stops it from being removed. The pupils need time to *apply* their new ideas, and make them a part of their global and useable understanding. At KS1/2 we can ask them about the cycling of other simpler materials, as in the case study about rubbish in Chapter 3. Such experiences are needed to enable an understanding that what we see as coming and going (the growth and burning of a tree) can be explained as the conservation of the atoms involved.

Often pupils can read texts and answer questions without understanding – simply repeating words from the text back as their answers to questions.

Techniques that give pupils the opportunity to **interact with the text** they are reading are often called *Directed Activities Related to Texts* (DARTs). In essence they give pupils the chance to think and reflect about what they are reading. The commonest examples are Cloze procedures where gaps are left in the text, but more demanding are

- scrambled texts which have to have their paragraphs re-ordered
- diagram labelling (from descriptions in text)
- card sorting (and cut and paste exercises)
- underlining or marking texts (using photocopies they can keep)

Figure 1.2 DARTs

Any written work usually goes through several drafts before going to press. The first 'draft' is likely to be a verbal discussion about what you intend to say. Writing in school science needs to go through the same process – begin by asking the pupils to tell each other what they predict, what they saw, what happened, etc. They are then able to express themselves in their writing – **Creative writing**.

The important factor is the **audience**. Pupils writing for the teacher as examiner will wonder if they 'have got it right'. But if they are writing for a newspaper, their younger sibling, the class that follows, or a web page, their sense of ownership gives them confidence to write what they really understand and believe. This may, of course, contain misconceptions – and creative writing is a good elicitation technique too – but better they expose their misconceptions early than produce writing that isn't theirs and they don't understand.

Learning logs are written for the learner themselves as audience. Examples have been given in Figure 1.1. They allow a degree of honesty from the learner.

Concept maps. These are also constructed for the learner themselves as audience and can be very powerful learning tools. Figure 1.4 is a type of concept map of constructivist learning.

Figure 1.3 Creative writing

Many schemes of work revisit science ideas every two years – by which time many pupils have forgotten the ideas from first time round. Unless ideas are used all the time they are not going to be felt important by children. So once our idea (that matter doesn't come and go at will) is seeded, we need to use it continually with the children. One question, one comment a week, that's all it takes. And this is only possible if the ideas are firmly a part of the teacher's outlook too.

This process is illustrated in simplified form in Figure 1.4.

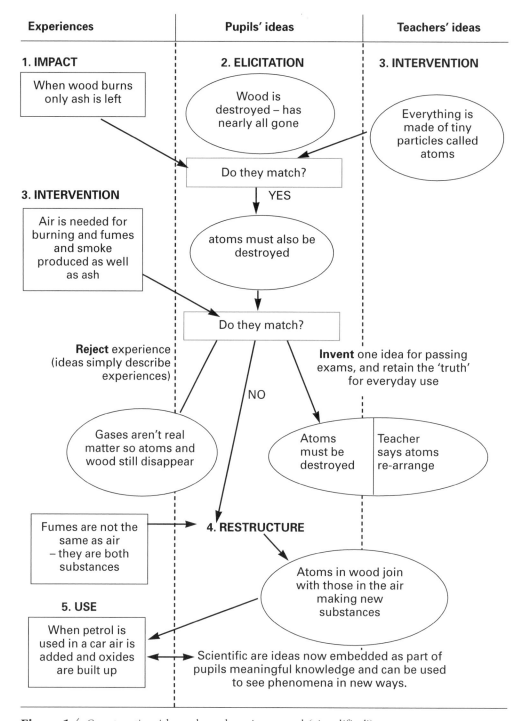

Figure 1.4 Constructing ideas about burning wood (simplified!)

Conservation at KS2

The exemplar sequence above was for pupils who should already have an understanding of conservation of matter in simpler situations such as the water cycle, dissolving or the idea that gases are real matter and have a weight. At primary school they need to focus on materials 'disappearing', such as puddles drying up, salt dissolving or balloons being blown up but seemingly getting lighter. Our intervention could be to collect condensation from evaporating water, evaporate or taste the salty water or to weigh the balloon before and after blowing air into it.

Atomic explanations (see Chapter 5) are appropriate at KS3 and 4, but even in the primary school children have heard of atoms, and we need to begin to give them an idea that they are not just little bits of ordinary matter. The important idea here is that the atoms within matter do not change, they simply join up in a different way. The Lego analogy is a good one – when you convert a Lego garage into a Lego house, the garage is destroyed and the house appears, but the bricks (building blocks or atoms) remain unchanged, they just join in a different way. This special property of atoms as unchanging was unrecognised by some of our teachers in training (Figure 1.1). Children come gradually to this idea of conservation, and an early model that explains what might be going on can help enormously in giving them this conservation view of the materials in their world in which change seems to be the rule.

Practical work

Pupils spend a considerable amount of time in their science in school doing investigative work. As teachers we need to make its purpose clear, otherwise it can become an aimless process of following a recipe. Sutton (1992, p. 2) points to the problem of:

> ensuring that the practical activities will be adequately embedded in a process of grappling with scientific ideas, but more generally there remains a problem of connecting practical work with the discussion and appreciation of ideas . . . and the description of WORD WORK as the core of a science lesson.

Each of the stages of the constructivist approach to teaching and learning described above can be supported by experiences and investigative work but it is vital that their purpose is clear to both teacher and learner:

- experiencing a phenomenon – used for impact, or eliciting pupils' ideas;
- illustrations – used for intervention, to get pupils to see things they haven't noticed before;
- investigating – used to test ideas, reformulate ideas or put them to use.

The first two may appear to be very much 'recipe' sessions where you give instructions of what to do. But this is justified because of the word-work that follows from them. Investigations should be more in the control of the learners themselves, though considerable support may also be given.

Towards scientific literacy

Meaningful learning must address our deep knowledge and understanding – it must not be a veneer. We claim that the approach to teaching we develop in this book focuses on the big ideas of science linked to everyday situations and the way they often conflict with the naive view. An education in science should be a support for life, and should open a new way of seeing the world.

Chapter 2

Science and the environment

Michael Littledyke

As outlined in the introduction, the purpose of this book is to demonstrate how primary science can be harnessed to support environmental education with the aim of producing environmentally literate, caring and responsible adults. These qualities are a prerequisite for a society that has any chance of achieving sustainability and long-term survival. And achieving them must be a primary aim of education on a planet which is suffering from ever increasing environmental degradation.

However, before we look at how this may be achieved, in the next two chapters we will consider the impact of science on the environment and perspectives on the environment through a summary of some of the key features in the history of science. In this chapter we examine how views of science have changed since the seventeenth century, while in the following chapter we show how environmentalist views which support the environment have developed. The intention here is to provide a historical backdrop which will help us to understand how early perspectives in science may have had profound influence in promoting environmentally damaging attitudes and how, in opposition, more positive environmentally supportive models have emerged.

The rationale for this approach is that understanding of the nature of science and scientific knowledge has an important influence on how science is taught (Harlen 1992) and several research studies have confirmed this connection (Lantz and Kass 1987; Duschl and Wright 1989; Brickhouse 1991, Lakin and Wellington 1994). This can also have direct impact on approaches to environmental education, affecting attitudes and understanding of the environment in pupils (Littledyke 1997a). One of our important tasks here, as reflective teachers, is to challenge our own assumptions and to improve our understanding of the influences which may have shaped our own attitudes, as these assumptions will be transmitted in teaching. An examination of features of the history of science is the best way to expose the influences of science on society and the environment, and hence on ourselves; to understand our present we must look to the past.

We will begin, then, in the historical and philosophical realm and see how the old beliefs of the medieval period were replaced by 'modern' science, which in turn has been overturned by 'postmodern' developments. 'Modern' science refers to the model of science produced at the time of the Enlightenment and prominent until the twentieth century. This model aspires to an objective and ultimately complete understanding of the universe. The 'modern' model has been superseded by 'postmodern' developments in science which acknowledge that scientific knowledge changes with new forms of evidence and that objectively accurate and complete descriptions of the world are not possible in an absolute sense. In this chapter we will trace important features of the history of these changes.

Varying views of science

The advantages of science are self-evident, as it has produced innumerable developments through its application in technology. This has led to improved health and higher economic standards, resulting in generally enhanced living conditions for large numbers of people across the world. Appleyard explains this by equating science with a capacity to change and manipulate the world to our advantage, and considers that 'science provides a way of knowing and doing almost anything we like . . . It is conceptually and technologically effective' (1992, p.6). Its political and economic significance is well understood by politicians as exemplified by Nehru who spoke for governments across the globe when he famously said that 'the future belongs to science and those who make friends with science' (cited in Hawking 1988, p.175). This potential for control assumes almost a status of deity in Hawking's view of science which sees no boundaries to the potentials of scientific discovery, considering science to be fundamental to understanding of the universe and proposing the possibility of a complete theory which unifies space and time; within this view of science lies the key to unlocking the ultimate secrets of existence:

> . . . then we shall all, philosophers, scientists and just ordinary people, be able to take part in the discussion of why it is that we and the universe exist. If we find the answer to that it would be the ultimate triumph of human reason, for then we should know the mind of God. (1988, p. 175)

Other writers, including many literary figures, have been more critical of science. Tolstoy, for example, considers science to be meaningless to human purpose: 'Science is meaningless because it gives no answer to our question, the only important question, important for us: "What shall we do and how shall we be?"' (cited in Wolpert 1992, p. 144). Whilst D. H. Lawrence sees science as sterile and abstract: 'Knowledge has killed the sun, making it a ball of gas with spots . . . The world of reason and science . . . this is the dry and sterile world that the abstracted mind inhabits' (cited in Wolpert 1992, p. ix). Wittgenstein, the towering 20th century philosopher, echoes these views of the limitations of science when he states: 'We feel, that even when all scientific questions have been answered, the problems of life remain completely untouched' (1951, p. 187).

These critical views point to a more destructive aspect to science, which is encapsulated by Vaclav Havel, who sees science as the conqueror and destroyer of nature:

> Modern science . . . abolishes as mere fiction the innermost foundations of our natural world: it kills God and takes his [*sic*] place on the vacant throne so henceforth it would be science that would hold the order of being in its hand as its sole legitimate guardian and so be the legitimate arbiter of all relevant truth . . . People thought they could explain and conquer nature – yet the outcome is that they destroyed it and disinherited themselves from it. (cited in Wolpert 1992, p. ix)

How, then, can such vastly contradictory views of science coexist? To understand this we must look at some key features in the history of scientific development, and, as we do this, the contradictions will become evident.

The rise of science

The history of science is a fascinating and important narrative which is crucial to understanding how views of science and its widespread effect on society have changed. Only a summarised account of some of the important features is possible here, though Appleyard (1992) provides a more detailed analysis of the critical stages, whilst Losee (1993) provides details of the philosophy of the key scientific figures.

It is not commonly realised that science was developed and applied in North African and Middle Eastern Muslim culture from around the eighth century, something that has been largely ignored by Christian dominated historical analysis (Butt 1991). The usual account provided by Western historians is that science emerged (in Europe) in the sixteenth and seventeenth century as a rational response to the previous dominance of religious faith and superstition of the medieval period. The European medieval period was characterised by the authority and dominance of the church in social and political life, while people also looked to folklore, superstition and magic to help them understand the world. Medieval Catholicism was strongly influenced by St Thomas Aquinas's *Summa Theologica* of 1266, which refined some of the earlier ideas of Aristotle, and which gave an intellectual basis for Christianity. This saw:

- the Earth at the centre of the universe; all changeable, lumpish heavy matter had found its way to the centre;
- the heavens as perfect and made of celestial matter;
- humans living on the Earth in the midst of change and decay, but with the possibility of salvation through Christ; thus we alternated between animals and angels; human existence is seen as a stepping stone to God (as symbolised by magnificent Gothic cathedrals which rise and aspire to the heavens, signifying the transcendent and eminent nature of God);

- knowledge as based on faith and authority of the divine message as given through the gospels and the church;
- God as the designer of creation with 'man (sic) created in His likeness';
- the role of reason as to interpret ways of following God's plan on Earth with the goal of salvation.

There were a number of major challenges to these medieval views. Columbus (1492) 'discovered' America and showed that the Earth was round. This also exposed areas which were not known. Previously the known world was thought to be finite, and ideas were defined and confined by the doctrines of religion and drew boundaries to knowledge. The new findings opened up boundaries and the idea of radical doubt and limited knowledge emerged. Copernicus (1473–1543) showed that the planets revolved around the sun (heliocentrism), displacing the Earth at the centre of the universe (geocentrism). Humans were no longer at the centre of the universe and the idea of humans being the central purpose of the universe was now questioned. Galileo (1564–1642) showed through the telescope that the universe was bigger than was thought. The earth was seen to 'shine' by secondary illumination of the moon, showing it to be like other planets; new stars were observed; the heavens were not as Aristotle had described. Science as rational enquiry threatened the authority of the church. Galileo, as a leading edge in this irresistible movement, was seen as a dangerous heretic when he wrote: 'In science the authority embodied in the opinion of thousands is not worth the spark of reason in one man' (Appleyard 1992, p. 36). Aristotle and Aquinas had defined the boundaries of the universe, with the details of the map described through reason. Now the map was questioned. This heresy threatened the authority of the church and the foundation of faith. How much more was not known?

Scientific tools were developed, including mathematical skills and technological tools for observing and measuring, including telescopes, microscopes and clocks. Bacon (1561–1626), in his first documented accounts of scientific method, proposed stages of experimentation based on observation and practical investigation to establish facts which can then be used to generate general laws. The process refers to use of evidence, meticulous observation and enquiry to inform judgements. Descartes (1596–1650) proposed a philosophy of dualism. This separated soul and rationality, reason and passion, mind and matter. The Cartesian motto: 'Cogito, ergo sum' (I think therefore I am) proposed an observer of the universe (an 'I') which also observes the act of observing (consciousness or self awareness); non-humans were seen to be unaware and likened to machines. The four essentials of the scientific method were described:

- accept what is clear to the mind (i.e. rational)
- break larger problems to smaller (reduction)
- argue from simple to complex (induction)
- check from evidence.

From this all was called into doubt and stimulated the rise of scepticism and individualism. This was further aggravated by major sociopolitical change; economic wars (e.g. Anglo-Dutch wars) and the rise of nationalism replaced religious wars; capitalism with its individual opportunity replaced feudal authority; ideas of pragmatism and practicality became important, thus prudence survived but religious truth was relegated.

Newton (1642–1727) described universal laws of motion and gravity. This used the principle of algorithmic compression, that is, from observed patterns we can describe the whole. Newton's mechanics heralded a view of a clockwork universe driven by laws of physics and cause and effect; a reductionist view of the universe in which science would ultimately discover everything through the search for universal truths. This contrasted starkly with the medieval world-view, influenced by Aristotle's philosophy, which described a world of discrete objects which is not compressible and in which divine purpose, which was ultimately mysterious, was dominant. Science and religion were seen as separate and different views of the universe. The philosophy of dualism was firmly established and the Enlightenment had arrived; reason was all-powerful, and human conditions could be improved through its application.

The church's authority was well and truly undermined in the 19th century when Darwin proposed the theory of evolution by the process of natural selection. This showed humans as arising from ancestral animal forms and indicated chance as more significant than divine design in the forms of species. The idea of humans as being the main purpose of the universe was questioned further, as humans were now seen as not separately created from other animals, but a mere twig on a very bushy tree of evolution. There were obvious links between humans and chimps, who are noticeably very sexually active and promiscuous in their relationships. This was also very provocative to a Victorian morality which considered that 'young ladies should refrain from examining the sexual parts of flowers in case they are tainted'. In fact, Linnaeus, who earlier had devised the system of taxonomy for classifying living things, wanted to put chimps in the same genus as humans but considered it to be too provocative (Rousseau had done this previously, but others wanted to put humans in a separate kingdom). Darwin put humans in the same order (primates) as a compromise. The medieval view of humans as the centre and purpose of the universe was by now well and truly overturned.

A summary of the changes associated with the rise of rationality resulting from the Renaissance period (moving from the Medieval period), the period of the Enlightenment and beyond follows:

Medieval religious view	*post-Enlightenment non-religious view*
• geocentrism	• heliocentrism
• humans as the central purpose of the universe	• a purposeless mechanical universe
• humans as part of a divine order	• humans as chance products of evolution

- authority and faith dominate
- certainty of divine truth
- feudal system based on hierarchy and social order
- morality
- meaning through religion

- reason dominates
- doubt and scepticism
- capitalism based on individualism and economic opportunity
- neutrality, value free stance
- crisis of meaning

Twentieth century developments in science

Developments in twentieth century science have refined and extended the earlier scientific ideas in some cases, but have superseded and overturned them in others. Along with this a number of new scientific disciplines have emerged in which the medieval view of humans as the centre and purpose of existence, has transformed to a position where humanity is a mere player in a complex web of existence.

It should be said that some of these new ideas are very challenging and difficult to understand because they contradict our normal 'common sense' experience (though earlier scientific ideas, such as Newton's laws of motion can be counter-intuitive also). However, it is useful to have an overview of these recent ideas as they offer an essential critical perspective on science's contribution to our understanding of how we construct our relationship with the environment.

Ecology

The principles of energy degradation and cycling of matter show the dynamic processes at work in ecosystems. Energy and matter are related in living systems: photosynthesis transfers solar energy to chemical; respiration further transfers the energy in a form that can be used in cells to organise and maintain their structure and function; atoms are cycled through synthesis of sugars in photosynthesis and their conversion to carbon dioxide in respiration, with decay also contributing to the cycles. Principles of adaptation arising from complex relationships between species show how natural selection and evolution operates (for example, predator–prey evolution is interactive; as prey get faster to escape, so do predators to catch them). These ecological relationships show how change through evolutionary and ecological adaptation connects all living things. The relationships are finely balanced and fragile, however, and they are very susceptible to damage. The implications are that humans are a part of a complex web of ecological relationships in which we rely on the natural world for our existence and support, but also have the capacity to change and destroy it.

Genetics and 'neo-Darwinism'

Darwin showed how natural selection results in change and evolution. Genetics gave the basis for the mechanism through identifying genes as inheritable characters. These can vary in a population through mutations (random changes in the genetic code) and mixing through sexual combination. Natural selection as 'survival of the fittest' ensures that organisms are closely matched to the conditions in which they live. Significantly, DNA is the chemical molecule of inheritance which is common to all life forms on the planet. In fact, we share many of the DNA sequences with bacteria (and all other life forms) because we have similar metabolic functions at the cellular level, even though the forms are very different. We also share more than 98 per cent of genes with chimps, which, according to some taxonomic systems, makes us a third species of chimpanzee (Sagan and Druyan 1993). This confirms that humans are very much related to other living things through evolution and have not been separately created.

Natural selection principles have also been applied to physics and cosmology to produce a larger picture of evolution from the 'Big Bang', through a series of changes from subatomic particles to atoms to molecules within large scale organisations in the galaxies of innumerable stars and planets. In this picture our Earth is a minute part in a universe of incomprehensible vastness. All this shows that human evolution can be seen as a part of a continuum from the origins of life and previously from earlier evolving physical complexity beginning with the 'Big Bang'. It also shows that all living things are related, they are part of the same 'family', and there is a constant flow of material and energy between the living and non-living world which ultimately connects everything present and past.

Developments in 'new' physics

There have been a number of monumental theoretical developments in the twentieth century which have contradicted and overturned some central features of the Enlightenment model of physics described earlier. These ideas are inherently difficult to grasp from our everyday sense perspective, and point to a very strange universe in which we construct a particular human perspective from animal senses which have evolved to select and limit essential features from a complex environment.

Newton's mechanics were originally applied to large-scale events, such as the movements of objects on Earth and the movements of the planets. Newton's ideas have now been largely superseded by relativity theory, which is concerned with very large-scale and very fast phenomena; and quantum mechanics, which essentially involves the science of the very small, though Newton's mechanics remain a good approximation for human scale phenomena. It is not appropriate to go into details here, though summaries of these fascinating ideas are to be found in a number of books, such as Bohm (1983), Capra (1975), Davies (1983), Hawking (1988). There are, however, certain important philosophical implications to be drawn from the findings of twentieth century physics:

- the observer influences the state of the observed i.e. there is no independent reality that can be observed outside of the observer;
- the observed can never *fully* be known;
- there are no absolute values, only probabilities;
- all aspects of the universe are interconnected at a deep level.

These recent scientific ideas run directly counter to Enlightenment science which once aspired to objectively describe all aspects of the universe: this is clearly no longer a feasible proposition.

The science of complexity

This is a newly defined science which has emerged from 'chaos theory' (Gleick 1988, Waldrop 1994). This developed from the observation that in non-linear mathematical equations small differences in starting points produce unpredictable changes in graphs when extended. The patterns resulting can be ordered, for example cyclical patterns, or can be chaotic, and the ideas have been applied to studies of many complex systems, such as the weather, changes in ecosystems and even to economics. The elements of a complex system are also subtly connected so that small changes in one part can have profound but unpredictable effects in another. This is the so called 'butterfly effect' in which the flap of a butterfly's wings in one part of the world could trigger off a large weather change in another part through the multiplied and magnified effects as the changes get transferred (see Chapter 7).

The important idea that new levels of order can spontaneously emerge from complex systems has revolutionised the way we look at the world. A common example used to illustrate this is the sand pile; a new form, the pile, emerges when individual grains of sand are piled up on top of each other. The properties of the individual grains, which are rounded, are quite different from the pile, which has a mounded shape with unpredictable patterns of avalanches (chaos) and stability (order) as the grains pile up. Such emergent order is a feature of all complex systems with dynamically interacting elements. Fractals, for example, are repeating patterns of order which occur in mathematical and natural systems and have been used to explain such diverse structures as: the beautiful patterns in Mandelbrot sets which emerge from iterating (infinitely repeating) mathematical equations; repeating branching patterns in natural objects such as trees, branches, twigs; and complex patterns in social animals, such as swarms of fish, bird movements or termite nests, which result from repeated simple behaviour of individuals (Briggs 1992).

There are a number of important implications arising from the science of complexity:

- patterns of order exist in chaotic systems;
- there is a new approach to evolutionary theory since there is inherent order in dynamic systems with natural selection fine tuning the process – this supersedes the idea of random chance events being acted on by natural selection;
- there is evidence for deep order in the universe;
- there are implications for the understanding of humans and consciousness, in which consciousness may be an example of emergent order resulting from the interaction of nerve cells (see Dennett 1993; Pinker 1998);
- we see the limitations of a reductionist approach in science, and perceive that the properties of the whole are not merely the sum of the parts. (See

Chapter 5 in which the properties of atoms are shown to be quite different from the 'real' objects which are made up of them.)

These twentieth century findings of science point to a universe which is vastly different from the earlier mechanical model of the Enlightenment. However, the earlier model has had enormous influence on Western thought. We will, therefore, now consider how some of these important historical changes and developments in science have implications for understanding the impact of science on the environment.

Science and attitudes to the environment

17th century and post-Enlightenment scientific views have had great influence on society. These views were rooted in the following:

- objectivity, that is science provides an emotionally distanced and accurate view of reality;
- dualism, that is the separation of mind and matter, reason and emotion, which is needed for objectivity;
- rationality, that is the world can only be known through reason and this will lead to knowing it fully;
- a neutral, value free stance, which is needed to achieve objective truth;
- reductionism, that is, science can know the whole by reducing it to its parts;
- a mechanical view of the universe, in which reductionism will describe the parts;
- positive realism, that is science is an approach to absolute truth which describes the real world independently of humans.

Our journey through some of the important historical developments in science has demonstrated that these views have been questioned, and some would say completely overturned by twentieth century science. However, these ideas are particularly significant when we look at how society has damaged the environment.

Modern and postmodern approaches to science

The features of Enlightenment science have been characterised as a central component of the so-called 'modern' world-view:

> Generally perceived as positivistic, technocentric and rationalistic, universal modernism has been identified with the belief in linear progress, absolute truths, the rational planning of ideal social orders, and the standardisation of knowledge and production (Precis 6, quoted in Harvey, 1989, p. 9)

The 'project' of modernity is generally recognised as covering the period from the seventeenth century to the last quarter of the twentieth century and is closely associated with the development of objective science during the Enlightenment as a means of understanding the universe. Universal morality and law were defined as a way of following its rules, and autonomous art was a way of reflecting its inner harmony and logic. The idea was to use knowledge to control nature, to remove want and to liberate human thought from the irrationalities of superstition, myth and religion (Littledyke 1996).

Postmodern writers such as Lyotard, Derrida, Baudrillard, Foucault, Rorty and others have criticised these assumptions, concluding that the pursuit of universal, permanent truths is illusionary, as all knowledge is limited by language and is inherently culturally bound (Lyon 1994). This approach, sometimes called *deconstructive* postmodernism, challenges the notion of a meta-language, meta-narrative or meta-theory which explains and connects things. The deconstructive postmodern position, therefore, seeks to identify the values and cultural assumptions in ideas, and this inevitably gives rise to multiple interpretations and understandings; implying the death of so-called 'grand theory'. This is embodied in the statement of Rorty: 'for those who espouse a postmodern perspective, reality is nothing but a temporary text constructed out of other texts' (1982, p. 15). In this approach a scientific view has no more validity as an approach to reality than other views, religious, aesthetic, ethical or cultural.

Constructive or *revisionary* postmodernism, in contrast, seeks to revise modern concepts to construct: 'a new unity of scientific, ethical, aesthetic and religious institutions. It rejects not science as such but only that scientism in which the data of the modern sciences are alone allowed to contribute to the construction of our world-view' (Griffin, 1988, p. x).

This acknowledges the limitations of the 'modern' world-view but emphasises that important features, including scientific knowledge, must not be lost but revised and incorporated into a new emancipatory world view taking into account the revolutionary twentieth century developments in science. This also implies that the modern mechanistic paradigm is replaced by what some authors refer to as a more ecological (Birch 1988; Ferre 1988) or 'organicist' (Griffin 1988) one, which is more likely to achieve sustainable relationships with the environment. Constructive postmodernism, in contrast to deconstructive post-modernism, is, therefore, compatible with current science as it offers a critical understanding of the limitations and environmentally destructive influences of modern science, whilst accepting the more ecologically compatible findings of twentieth century science.

The influences of the modern science

We return now to consider some of the unfortunate consequences of the 'modern' view of science before looking to the future with more hope.

While the rise of science transformed the world and produced undoubted improvements to social conditions, the modern, Enlightenment model of science has been implicated in the ecological crisis arising from its application through technology (Roszak 1970; Fox 1990; Naess 1989; Sessions 1974; Drengson 1989), leading to what Diamond (1992) refers to as the sixth major extinction period, in which over half of existing species are likely to be extinct by the middle of the next century. Previous major extinction periods, the most recent resulting in the demise of the dinosaurs, were probably due to physical effects (including meteor impact or volcanic activity), but this present period is uniquely related directly to the activities of one particular species. The success of *Homo sapiens* lies in its ability to exploit the resources of its environment to its own end. However, the inventiveness of the means to do this through technology and the ever increasing scale of the impact has drawn this species to the brink of its own potential destruction along with vast numbers of others. Whilst the sources of this crisis are complex and extend far into human evolutionary history (Sagan and Druyan 1993), the impact of the application of modern science on the environment has been undoubtedly devastating.

Objectification and 'modern' science

Swimme (1988) considers that modern science has contributed significantly to militaristic, patriarchal, anthropocentric and Eurocentric dominance through its impact socially, ethically, technologically and environmentally and its position as the dominant paradigm for some three hundred years. The key to these problems lie in objectification, which is the central theme in this model of science.

Monod typifies 'modern' scientists' support for objectification by his statement that 'science depends upon the postulate of objectivity' (1972, p. 30). However, the process of distancing through objectification also disengages feelings and ethics, creating the conditions for exploitation and domination. This has been a common feature of the application of science to the natural environment. Bacon, who is regarded as a very important figure in the early development of science, illustrates this explicitly in his use of images of brutality and force in his scientific approach to nature, which were drawn from the interrogation and persecutions of witches, when he wrote in his *De Dignitate et Augementis Scientarium* (1623):

> The way in which witchcraft, magic, and all superstitions are prosecuted and run aground . . . not only sheds useful light on how people accused of such things should be treated, but we can also borrow from it useful directions for unveiling nature's secrets. No one need have scruples about penetrating these caverns and corners when interrogating the truth is his only object. (cited in Merchant 1980, p. 168)

In another of his works, *Novum Organum* (1620), he argued: 'The new interrogation method leads to the analysis and dismemberment of nature. The spirit provides the suggestions and the hands do the work. In this way human knowledge and human power are one.' (cited in Merchant 1980, p. 171) He encouraged scientists to subdue and enslave nature, and concluded that in this way its secrets would be discovered and humanity would achieve control over it. This approach set the scene for subsequent application of science for over three hundred years. In the process, patterns of objectification have produced alienated views and destructive practices towards the environment.

Thus, obedience and control (of nature), as the aim of Enlightenment science, are associated with a mechanistic world-view (machines are instruments of human control), and these are integral to many social structures. An extreme example of how attitudes may be shaped by these processes is provided by the training of soldiers. Humphrey (1993) discusses how objectification and insensitivity to suffering of others is a requisite for inflicting suffering. To achieve this, soldiers are often trained in conditions of humiliation with the discrediting of the person as an individual and the suppression of feelings. This is necessary to carrying out orders which involve actions which would normally be repugnant, such as killing people:

> Overriding all other issues is a strong racist flavour that pervades the attitude of the military . . . An essential element in most massacres or atrocities is a preceding psychological step in which victims are relabelled and identified as being different, inferior or even subhuman, which allows (the soldier) to commit acts that would be unthinkable if the victims were viewed as human beings like him. (Bourne 1971, cited in Humphrey, p. 99)

People are clearly prone to distancing themselves from the effects of their actions, as is illustrated by Milgram's famous study on 'obedience to authority' (1974), which involved experimental subjects who were instructed by 'scientists' (who were actually actors) to inflict apparent electric shocks on a subject supposedly to investigate learning processes. Remarkably, 65 per cent of the subjects were prepared to administer shocks up to 450 volts under instructions of a 'researcher', showing that humans have a great capacity for inflicting damage when they absolve themselves of responsibility through the 'objective' position of scientific research.

The training of soldiers is an overt example of how destructive behaviour can be shaped. Foucault's analysis of discipline and punishment shows that discipline 'dissociates power from the body . . . it reverses the course of the energy, the power that might result from it, and turns it into a relation of strict subjection' (1977, p. 138). He describes how discipline practices were once externalised in the form of public punishments (e.g. hangings and floggings) but have now become more subtly internalised into social institutions. Thus training procedures in businesses, the police, schools, etc. may foster objectification processes so that workers may engage in various destructive practices, such as polluting technologies or weapons manufacture, because they absolve themselves of responsibility for any destructive effects.

The discipline of science has had a key role in this process of disconnection from the consequences of action. Eagan and Orr (1992) discuss how modern science education can implicitly reflect values which are alienated from nature, in that a formal curriculum which prioritises abstract ideas will disconnect people from nature. Such objectification processes are common in relationships with the environment. When living things are seen as objects of use or of no consequence then permission is available to destroy them. When this attitude is also linked with anthropocentrism, where human concerns are seen to be of greatest significance, then this creates potent conditions for environmental exploitation. This view is summarised by White in his rejection of anthropocentrism when he argues that Christianity has a burden of 'guilt' for ecological problems which are translations of the dogma of humanity's rightful mastery over nature. He contends that:

> We deserve our increasing pollution because, according to our structure of values, so many other things have priority over achieving a viable ecology. The problem with our structure of values is that a man-nature dualism is deep rooted in us . . . Until it is eradicated not only from our minds but also from our emotions, we shall doubtless be unable to make fundamental changes in our attitudes and actions affecting ecology.
> (White 1967, cited in Fox, 1990, p. 7)

Influences of the 'modern' model of science on science education

The history of science demonstrates that scientific ideas develop and change through new evidence and scientific debate, sometimes leading to major paradigm shifts in thinking (Kuhn 1970). In this way twentieth century science has superseded the earlier scientific models of the Enlightenment; the post-modern has superseded the modern. However, limitations of teachers in their understanding of the nature of science can have a significant influence in how science is taught, and the positivist ideas of many teachers (Clayden *et al.* 1994; Littledyke 1997a) and their lack of understanding of the nature and history of science (Lakin and Wellington 1994) contributes to the perpetuation of modern approaches. This may lead to inappropriate personal models of science and inappropriate teaching methods which may also lead to objectification of the environment.

In such models science is seen as skills and principles to be learnt with teaching designed to demonstrate the skills and 'prove' the principles. In this commonly held model science is conveyed as:

- objective;
- capable of yielding ultimate truths;
- proving things;
- having a defined and unique subject matter;
- having unique methods;
- being value free. (Harlen 1992, p. 2)

This essentially 'modern' view of science assumes that scientists uncover scientific 'truths' through scientific research and science education is designed to teach these 'truths'. Individual constructions of meaning from these 'truths' are seen as more or less accurate means of understanding defined scientific principles. This creates a hierarchy of 'correct' views and misconceptions. Teaching methods derived from such views see the locus of control for learning as being outside the learner, with the aims of teaching as an induction process into 'correct' understanding. Thus, 'correct' ideas are located in scientific theories communicated or demonstrated by teachers, secondary resources or activities which illustrate principles. Teacher direction and liberal use of instructions through work cards would typify such an approach at the primary level.

However, an examination of the history of science shows that knowledge is tentative rather than fixed, leading to an understanding of science as a process of testing ideas to develop provisional theories of natural phenomena. Thus, scientific knowledge as it can be 'known' has a permanent conjectural nature (Popper 1963). Furthermore, construction of science takes place in a social context and this influences the nature of that knowledge and the processes by which it was constructed (Kuhn 1970; Medawar 1979). This view of science as a process of the generation of tentative and provisional ideas will produce a pedagogy which develops scientific understanding through the testing of ideas against evidence, with the ideas being as good as the evidence which supports them. Science teaching will thus emphasise exploration of ideas with alternative ideas examined in the light of supporting evidence. In this model science will be conveyed as:

- human endeavour to understand the physical world;
- producing knowledge which is tentative, always subject to challenge by further evidence;
- building upon, but not accepting uncritically, previous knowledge and understanding;
- a social enterprise whose conclusions are often subject to social acceptability;
- constrained by values (Harlen 1992, pp. 2–3)

This is a more appropriate model of science and is more in keeping with constructive postmodern twentieth century views of science.

Science education for an environmentally sustainable postmodern world

To achieve environmental sustainability it is essential that the outmoded modern model of science is exposed for its contribution to objectification and damage of the environment and a more appropriate postmodern model is substituted. The main aims of such a model would be:

To develop cognitive modes in science, in order to:

- educate children into the methods and ideas of science so that they can use science to understand the world around them;
- assist children in creating meaningful personal frameworks for understanding science so they can apply scientific knowledge to informing personal lifestyle choices and political actions which will sustain the environment;
- critically analyse ideas and the application of ideas for scientific validity so they can develop a balanced view of the complexities of environmental options;
- critically evaluate the social and environmental implications of the application of scientific ideas.

Also to develop affective modes, to:

- foster a sense of interest, enjoyment and excitement in learning in science, so that they incorporate the methods and ideas of science into their view of the world;
- include a sense of beauty, respect, reverence and awe in approaches to the environment and understanding our place in the universe;
- develop an empathy with living things and the environment in general from the understanding that all living and non-living things are subtly interconnected and related through cycles of change and evolution;
- encourage a desire for appropriate action which will support the environment.

This book is dedicated to achieving these aims. However, before we examine how the science curriculum can be used for this purpose, we look, in the next chapter, at how views of the environment have developed and the implications for environmental education.

Chapter 3

Environmentalism and environmental education

Michael Littledyke

In Chapter 2 we explored the relationship between science and the environment through an examination of certain key stages in the history of western science. In this chapter we will look at how views of nature have developed: the emergence of environmentalism, as an approach which questions the damaging effects of science and technology and seeks sustainable alternatives, is a direct reaction to the environmental excesses of industrial society. We will examine these ideas and outline the implications for science and environmental education.

Anthropocentrism: mastery and control of nature

The analysis in the previous chapter showed that objectification processes inherent in modern science as it developed since the Enlightenment have contributed to exploitive attitudes and environmentally damaging technological practices. The core of this is the desire to ensure human mastery over the natural world and the attitude that the natural environment is the property of humans to use as they wish. This is often referred to as anthropocentrism, which places humans at the pinnacle of the natural world in terms of importance, priority and dominance. The historical developments outlined in Chapter 2 show that these assumptions have been challenged and overthrown from within science itself; humans are but a small twig on the complex bush of evolution in which all living things are related; our planet is but a speck in an incomprehensibly vast universe. However, the core values of anthropocentrism remain dominant, as the environmental damage created by society continues and intensifies.

In the medieval and early 'modern' period religion has been implicated in developing anthropocentric values. For example, Thomas (1982) argues that Christian biblical teachings justify the placing of humans at the centre of creation; within this system all natural things were part of a natural order which had a divine purpose to provide for the needs of human beings. The superiority of humans was justified through their capacity for rational thought, political judgement, religious belief, the use of tools and science, and even the capacity for humour and laughter. This theme was also developed by White (1967) who emphasised the role of Judaeo-Christianity in separating human beings from nature by a hierarchical chain of being completed by humans at the top (a theme running throughout the Old Testament). Such a value system regards all parts of the natural world as available for exploitation for human gain; this view of nature as property lies at the source of environmental problems. It should also be recognised, however, that respect for nature can also be located in scriptures. It is inherent in Judaisms; and current Christian ethics regard humans' relationship with nature as a tenancy rather than freehold ownership, with nurturing rather than exploitive values and with stewardship as the dominant theme (Smith 1998).

Descartes, in the seventeenth century, established anthropocentrism within science by equating non-human animals to machines who were equipped with impulses and reflexes, but had no capacity for sensation, language, rational thought or suffering. This fully justifies the use of animals for hunting, domestication, vivisection, meat consumption, as well as large-scale activities such as mining and deforestation. This separation of humans from nature was also a part of the philosophy of Cartesian dualism which divided and prioritised mind over body, reason over emotion, subduing feeling and creating the conditions for nature's objectification and dispassionate mastery, control and exploitation.

The important point here is that the way in which views and values of nature are constructed within societies has influence on the actions of the society (Eder 1996). This translates directly into environmental impact. It should also be noted that the anthropocentric view contrasts sharply with that of many premodern tribal societies in that relationship and responsibility are of prime importance in such groups (Maybury-Lewis 1991). Such views are common to various tribal cultural/environmental relationships and are essentially spiritual and ecological perspectives. For example, Gough (1990, p. 16) discusses the 'human kinship with nature' highlighted by Aboriginal stories which show that 'the land that visiting Europeans and Americans still see as "empty" desert is shown to be brimming with life, with food for all who care to look for it'. In the premodern tribal worldview the world is seen as vitally and dynamically 'alive' with living things regarded as relatives, as well as offering the means for human existence. This contrasts directly with the environmentally alienated position of science in the modern era.

Concern for the environment

There is considerable evidence that many human societies have damaged their environments, particularly since the onset of agriculture and permanent settlements, though, as indicated above, earlier hunter gatherer societies tended to live more in balance with their ecosystems (Sagan and Druyan 1993). However, environmental damage has intensified to take on global proportions during the period of industrialisation and exponential population growth.

Smith (1998), discusses how, in industrial development, the environment could be mixed with human labour to create property, while ecosystems were also treated as a vast rubbish dump for human wastes and by-products of technology that could not be put to use. In relatively small populations the environment could, to a point, absorb this pollution, but as populations expanded and technological capacity intensified ecosystems were often damaged or fundamentally transformed. Such ecological changes predate the modern, industrial period; for example, the patchwork of the English landscape, which is now regarded as natural, was largely created by wood clearance for the construction of houses and ships and the transfer of the land to farming during the medieval period. However, the impact of the industrial revolution, with its demands for materials and labour, has affected the whole of the biosphere, so that now all aspects of the global environment have been affected through extensive pollution (for example, DDT has even been found in penguins in the Antarctic) and changes in the atmosphere (particularly, ozone depletion harming the vitally important barrier to harmful ultra-violet solar rays; and increased carbon dioxide levels causing global warming). This has led McKibbon (1990) to describe these pervasive changes as 'the end of nature', which he refers to as a biosphere which has been permanently changed by human activity and is no longer a 'natural' product of its own ecological activity.

Concern about the environment can be seen in the nineteenth century art and writings of Constable, Blake, Wordsworth, Coleridge, Ruskin and others. These views saw danger in encroaching industrialisation and its associated environmental degradation. Whereas in Britain much of the environment has already been changed through human intervention, so that the concept of what is natural landscape is somewhat problematic, in other countries preservation of uncontaminated wilderness was significant. Thoreau in his classic book *Walden* (1886) despised the environmentally damaging, materialistic and over-consumptive lifestyle of nineteenth century America, while calling for a new appreciation of the beauty of nature and an associated ethic which respects and preserves the natural environment. His powerful ecological and political statement has influenced environmentalist views to the present day.

However, Thoreau's calls for preservation of uncontaminated wilderness have been superseded later by an approach of environmental conservation, which includes prudent management of natural resources for present and future generations and an ethic of wise stewardship rather than exploitive ownership. Thus, the creation of carefully managed National Parks in the USA and other countries in the early twentieth century, with controlled access of the public, secured the continuation of selected wilderness. This was different from the preservationist approach of Thoreau, whose writings would imply restricted public access, plus a general simplification of lifestyle with reduced consumption of consumer goods to minimise impact on the environment as a whole.

In the mid twentieth century the limits to the conservationist approach were pointed out by Leopold (1949) who in his book *A Sand County Almanac* expressed concern for continuing environmental degradation and called for a new set of values for land in which 'love, respect and admiration' are of more significance than monetary values. However, by the 1960s and 1970s the effects of polluting technology on the environment were becoming increasingly evident. This was highlighted by Carson's highly influential book *Silent Spring* (1962), in which she showed how increasing use of agricultural pesticides, particularly DDT, were leading to pests becoming resistant to the effects of the chemicals, while concentration of the poisons in food chains was also causing damage to animals higher up the chain, resulting in, as is symbolised by the book's evocative title, the disappearance of certain birds in areas of high pesticide use. This heralded a period of increasing concern about the environment with further significant publications including; *The Limits to Growth* (Meadows *et al.* 1972), which demonstrated how human economic activities resulting in pollution and resource depletion were unsustainable for the capacity of the Earth; and the *Blueprint for Survival* (Goldsmith *et al.* 1972), which showed how fundamental changes in values were required if the Earth was to survive industrialism. The idea of the ecological sustainability of human activity was placed firmly on the agenda and has been the major source of debate to the present time. Precisely what constitutes sustainability is highly disputed, but there is common consensus that ever increasing pollution, habitat destruction and resource depletion is unsustainable in the long term, leading inevitably to environmental decay affecting ecological systems as well as human quality of life and even the survivability of our species.

The radical philosophy of 'deep ecology' was a response to these concerns (Fox 1990; Naess 1989; Sessions 1974; Drengson 1989). Deep ecology recognises intrinsic value in all living things and identifies anthropocentrism, or the prioritising of humans at the expense of other living things, as the central problem in environmental issues, in that 'insecure, acquisitive individualism is the most destructive of the narrow human viewpoint' (LaChapelle 1991, p. 18). Deep ecology, as 'the perception of reality as relationship' (Julien Puzey, cited in LaChapelle 1991, p. 18), offers ecological sustainability. This is contrasted with 'shallow environmentalism', described by Naess (1973) as the fight against pollution and resource depletion, which he criticises as essentially resource management with anthropocentric underpinnings. Implicit in the ideas of deep ecology is the model of small scale, localised economic activities, similar to those espoused by Schumacher in *Small is Beautiful* (1973). This model advocates Buddhist economics as a system which prioritises values within the relationship of human labour to the quality of life that it promotes, affecting the lives of people involved in work; consumers of the products; and the environment which provides the raw materials and absorbs potential waste. Such a system takes into account the total impact of economic activity, whilst endeavouring to preserve the quality of all the participants; producer, consumer and environment. This contrasts with our present economic system which holds monetary value as paramount, rewarding the owners of production while encouraging excessive, environmentally damaging consumption through the pursuit and construction of markets. (Though there have been some recent attempts to put a penalty value on pollution through such measures as increased fuel and transport tax, packaging laws and refuse tax.)

These developments raised the profile of the environment in the public and political arena leading to the emergence of an internationally organised environmental movement spearheaded by such organisations as Friends of the Earth and Greenpeace who have been successfully active in stimulating a series of environmental campaigns on specific issues to raise public awareness and to initiate political responses, including, for example: removal of lead from petrol (charged with causing brain damage in children); cessation of CFC use (implicated in ozone depletion); a ban on seal culling and international whaling, and making the wearing of animal furs unfashionable due to links with cruelty. As a result of such campaigns and increasing debate on the issues, concern about the environment has moved into the political mainstream, resulting in the environment being a major concern for the public domain, and taking priority in the main political party agendas (including the existence of the Green Party as a political party whose reason d'être is about protecting the environment).

Alongside this and within these environmental groups has been the emergence of environmental activists who have orchestrated publicity campaigns to raise awareness of environmental issues, being prepared, in some cases, to break the law to gain publicity for their ends. Groups such as Earth First, for example, have sometimes been described as eco-terrorists and have been known to damage machinery or drive metal spikes into trees making their felling and cutting by chain saw operators an extremely dangerous activity. However, such activities have drawn criticism from many quarters, including other environmentalists, who prefer more politically oriented or less dangerous tactics to achieve their ends. Nonetheless, there has been increasing activity to protect the environment undertaken by members of the public. For example, attempts to build roads through environmentally sensitive areas have drawn together a wide spectrum of people in direct opposition through petitions and encampments aimed at preventing the construction. At the same time, consumer action to boycott products of concern, such as genetically modified foods, has stimulated policy changes in retail outlets to meet the demands, as well as considerable debate at government level. As well as this direct action there is a general recognition of the need for consumer action to protect the environment and increasing numbers of people participate in numerous ways, for example: sales and demand for organic food continue to grow; numerous recycling centres have been set up across the country to receive tins, glass, paper and textiles, while local authorities have instigated schemes for house to house collection (encouraged by a law which requires them to recycle a proportion of household waste). The general level of environmental awareness and action to protect the environment on a number of fronts has increased dramatically towards the end of the 20th century.

Support for environmental concern from science

Chapter 2 showed how 'modern' Enlightenment science promotes values and attitudes which, when applied, are inherently damaging to the environment. For this reason science can be viewed negatively and suspiciously by many members of the public. However, 'postmodern' scientific developments in the twentieth century have superseded 'modern' science and, significantly, point to ways in which environmental sustainabililty can be achieved. 'Postmodern' science offers support for concern for the environment by helping people to understand the issues concerned with environmental problems, by showing that humans are intrinsically in relation with the environment and also that altruistic behaviour which protects the environment is ultimately in everyone's interest. A central purpose of science education to support the environment is to develop these understandings and attitudes:

Understanding of environmental issues – we need to understand to make informed choices

Environmental problems resulting from pollution, habitat destruction and resource depletion have many complex dimensions which need to be fully considered to inform any action. Much of this book is concerned with how understanding of science concepts is important in understanding these issues; sociopolitical and economic issues are also relevant, while ethical issues underpin all of the factors. Children have great interest in such matters; they usually have a strong sense of fairness which they readily superimpose onto our dealings with the environment. In the classroom, discussion is needed to tease out the various factors and to question what are the likely advantages and disadvantages of forms of action which may affect the environment. Immediate and tangible contexts are the best starting points, for example: the effects of a local (or imaginary) building programme, or the choice of various consumer goods and resultant waste (which has impact on the environment through extraction of resources from the Earth, and from pollution in their production or disposal). In such discussions we may need to consider the effects of action on living things such as:

- individual animals (as in hunting, vivisection, use of animals in testing of chemicals or medical research which are objected to by animal rights protesters);
- a species (which may be rare or endangered);
- a sensitive ecosystem (which may be threatened);

or on the human environment:

- the social effects on people living in an area (will a development, or lack of it, enhance or reduce the quality of people's lives, and how?);
- the economy of the region (how will a development, or lack of it, affect jobs?)

Factors which are important to understand include:

- understanding relevant scientific concepts – for example, how fertilisers and pesticides improve food production through stimulating plant growth or preventing pest damage; principles of concentration of certain poisonous chemicals (such as DDT) through food chains and the effects on animals at the tops of chains, which may include humans (Chapter 8);
- considering the impact of particular activities on the environment through establishing chains of consequences – for example, car use involves consumption of finite resources and burning fossil fuels both in making the car and in driving it, while exhaust pollution contributes to increasing atmospheric carbon dioxide, linked to global warming, and particulates which affect asthma, particularly in children (Chapters 5 and 6);
- finding out about the life cycles of products to assess their environmental impact – for example, find out about the materials used in household waste and trace their origins in the Earth and routes in factory processing, use in shops and the options of dumping versus recycling (Chapter 5);
- weighing up evidence – for example, considering the benefits of chemicals in growing food against the possible damage to the environment or to health (Chapter 8);
- assessing risks – judging what are the risks of any potential harm and how important this may be; scientists commonly indicate risks of environmental impact, what is a high or low risk? (a 1 in 14 million chance of winning the lottery is a very low chance and such a figure applied to a predicted environmental impact would be very low risk, whereas a figure such as two from every five hospital beds include illness linked to smoking indicates that use of tobacco is a very high risk to health) (Chapter 9).

In working with primary children on these issues an appropriate level of language and complexity of detail needs to be found. Key Stage 1 children need starting contexts which are tangible and immediate, such as playground rubbish, while Key Stage 2 children are capable of dealing with surprising levels of complexity, responding with enthusiasm to complex social and environmental problems. Concept maps or annotated drawings are good ways of developing some of these ideas. Drama is also an excellent medium for exploring such problems (Littledyke 1998); two case study examples of this are included at the end of the chapter to illustrate this approach.

Relationship – we are all related and the universe is deeply interconnected

Anthropocentrism as a rational worldview is well and truly demolished by our understanding of evolution and our place in the universe. Although we may consider ourselves to be important, on the scale of evolution and ecology we are but a very small part of a very rich tapestry of planetary diversity (see Chapter 7), and while our success is largely due to our ability to manipulate the environment to our own ends, this could also be our downfall.

Knowledge of the deep relationship between all living things through shared ancestors, shared chemical processes, shared DNA and the constant recycling of matter between the living and non-living world shows that our present human form is on the one hand very recent in the history of life, and on the other hand transient and fluid in that we are constantly exchanging body chemicals through the intake of materials and the removal of wastes. Our body chemicals are changed countless times during our lives, even though the physical appearance is maintained. And what we are composed of at any time was once part of innumerable living and non-living things; the billions of atoms inside us were once part of countless other organisms and have been constantly recycled since their origins (in the early formation of stars in the case of carbon).

We humans, along with other mammals, are programmed to recognise and look after our immediate relatives. In particular, to care for children is an inbuilt biological imperative. This is true for most people at least, and even people who are capable of cruel and malicious acts, such as Nazi officers in concentration camps, are also known to show kindness to their friends and family. Science, however, tells us that our relatives actually extend to the whole of humanity and beyond that to include ultimately all of creation. When this model of relationship is fully understood it is likely to foster empathy, concern and a spiritual sense of connection with the world at large, which is an intrinsically environmentally friendly disposition. This relational world-view is seen by a number of authors (Bohm 1983; Capra 1975, 1982; Cobb 1988; Weber 1990) as offering a synthesis of scientific and religious views which draws on older, perhaps mystical views closer to Taoism or Buddhism, and which point to the interconnectedness of experience and the features of the universe. These are essentially spiritual and ecological perspectives and lie at the root of what is needed to guide action for environmental sustainability.

The relationship view of the world is supported by our current understanding of brain processes which also shows the anthropocentric view to be quite inappropriate, though it is understandable. Self-centredness is essential to all living things for their survival (Sagan and Druyan 1993). However, research into consciousness (for example Dennett 1992; Pinker 1998) indicates that this central sense of self is illusionary. Thought may be seen to be an emergent level of order which arises from the interaction of neural cells. This enables the brain to selectively interpret stimuli from the environment for its survival and brain processes can be seen to model features of the environment, self-awareness being a state in which the observer is also included in the model of the environment. Consciousness (as experience) is seen to be a process which involves interaction between stimuli, organisation and interpretation (in the brain). In this model perception and thought can be seen as a selective interpretation based on what is seen to be important and is dependent on memory and previous experience. Consciousness can therefore be compared to a virtual reality system rather than an accurate representation of the world. Anthropocentrism, which places the observer at the centre of the world, is a central part of the illusion.

Children can be introduced to these concepts of relationship by showing evolutionary links between animals as a branching bush of relationships, i.e. our relatives (as found in many textbooks, but simplified to show examples of the animal main groups); or as a time line represented by a long strip of paper around the room, divided into blocks of time since the formation of the Earth (some 5 billion years ago) and showing drawings and notes about living things alive at different points of the Earth's history, i.e. our ancestors. Children enjoy researching and drawing for these activities and it gives a very strong sense of the complexity of life on Earth as well as the idea of humans' very recent emergence on the scene.

Choice of action

Taking action on behalf of the environment may involve giving up something such as: taking a crowded bus instead of driving a comfortable car; supporting environmentally friendly products which often cost more; reducing energy consumption in the home by turning the heating thermostat down. Such actions are forms of altruism, which is a term used in a biological sense to describe actions where individuals are prepared to take action on behalf of others to the detriment of themselves. In the animal world it usually applies to such behaviour as parental care. In the case presented here it applies to action on behalf of the environment, as the more selfish alternatives can appear to be better options for the individual. Some form of altruistic behaviour is usually needed for environmental action. What has science to say about this?

The problem of altruism in evolutionary theory puzzled scientists for many years; if natural selection worked through survival of the fittest and the biological aim is to pass on one's own genes, how could behaviour which supports others have evolved? The answer came through the idea of shared genes in close relatives; parents will protect offspring because their own genes will survive if their offspring survive, while social animals with similar genes may also show such behaviour. Thus, bees in a colony which originate from one queen will be highly cooperative because they all share very similar genes whereas other social groups with degrees of genetic relationships, for example primate or human tribes, will show degrees of cooperation (Dawkins 1989). So-called game theory was developed to explain this problem, and mathematical models have been made to investigate choices for cooperation or competition/defection in animal interactions. The game, as a model for exploring cooperation vs. competition, is drawn from the 'Prisoner's Dilemma' (Poundstone 1992), in which two prisoners suspected of a crime are in separate cells with no form of contact and must decide whether to give evidence informing on their fellow conspirator (defect/cheat) or say nothing (cooperate with each other). The important question each must ask him/herself is what will my friend do? If both cooperate they get a small sentence (a reward effectively, seeing as they both committed the crime), if both cheat on each other they get a larger sentence, but below the maximum available because of incomplete evidence (a relatively small punishment), while if one cheats whereas the other cooperates the one who cheats goes free (a large reward) whilst the cooperator gets the maximum sentence for conviction of the full crime ('the sucker's payoff').

Cooperate or cheat?

This very effective game, drawing on the principles of game theory, can be organised with upper junior children to demonstrate the effects of cooperation or cheating.

Get into groups of three. One person is the banker and the other two are the players. Each player has two cards in each hand labelled COOPERATE and CHEAT. At the signal of the banker, who says 'play', each player puts one of the cards face down on the table. The banker now turns over the cards and gives out the winnings according to the cards shown and the four possible outcomes:

OUTCOME 1: Both played *cooperate*. The banker pays £300 – a reward for both players cooperating.

OUTCOME 2: Both played *cheat*. The banker fines each £10. This is punishment for both players cheating.

OUTCOME 3: Player A plays *cooperate* and player B plays *cheat*. The banker pays player B £500 (the temptation to cheat) and fines player A (the sucker) £100.

OUTCOME 4: Player A plays *cheat* and player B plays *cooperate*. The banker pays player A £500 (the temptation to cheat) and fines player B (the sucker) £100.

A summary of the outcomes is shown in Figure 3.1.

Play the game for 20 turns with the banker keeping the scores on a score sheet like the one which is shown in Figure 3.2. Repeat the game so that each person has a turn to be banker.

After playing the game so everyone has a turn to be banker and player it is important to hold a class discussion on what are the effects of different strategies in the game. Significantly, mutual cooperative strategies give the largest collective payoffs but there is an individual larger payoff for cheating when the other tries to cooperate, hence the temptation to cheat. In the one off situation of the prisoner's dilemma a risk analysis shows that the safest bet is to cheat, because the sucker's payoff is too large a penalty to risk. However, if the game is played many times the players may eventually realise that the best overall strategy is mutual cooperation because that gets the most from the bank (£600 – whilst the most that cheating can obtain is £400, i.e. £500 for the cheater, but a £100 fine for the sucker).

In evolution, mixed behaviour strategies of cooperation and competition will arise because a population of competitors is not stable because of fighting, which can be physically damaging, while a population of cooperators is open to cheating by defectors. When a computer competition was run, inviting contestants to submit their best strategy for the game (Axelrod 1984) the most successful strategy which produced the highest score against all others was called 'tit for tat'. This simple but effective strategy starts with cooperate then gives an identical response to whatever the opponent gave on the previous turn. Thus playing against a total cooperation strategy locks immediately into perpetual cooperation resulting in the maximum possible collective score

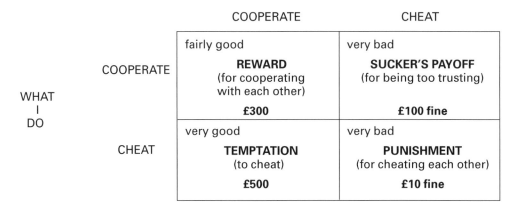

Figure 3.1 A summary of possible outcomes for 'Cooperate or Cheat?'

turn no	name: COOPERATE	CHEAT	PAYOFF	name: COOPERATE	CHEAT	PAYOFF
1						
2						
3						
4						
5						
6						
7						
8						
9						
10						
11						
12						
13						
14						
15						
16						
17						
18						
19						
20						
score						

Figure 3.2 Record chart for the banker to complete in 'Cooperate or Cheat?'

available from the bank; effectively both players win. However, whenever an opponent defects this causes 'tit for tat' to punish by defecting next time, while whenever the opponent cooperates 'tit for tat' rewarded by a similar response.

Glance and Huberman (1994) discuss how these ideas apply to human behaviour. In groups where people meet regularly cooperative behaviour is a mutual advantage to all. Tendencies of individuals to cheat are easily noticed in such groups and the behaviour is disapproved of or punished. In situations where people do not know each other well cheating may be easy to get away with. This is why close-knit tribal societies tend to be highly cooperative with a strong sense of group identity, cohesion and moral order, though there are also very strong pressures to conform to group norms, whilst more amorphous groups, as occurring in cities, show little collective identity and crime and social disorder is more prevalent. In the development of greatly populated human societies where individuals are less likely to know each other, the sense of responsibility must be directed towards more abstract concepts such as national identity, and laws regulating behaviour with a police, judiciary and penal system have arisen to ensure that cheaters are kept in line.

The very important message that game theory has, however, is that mutual cooperation is the best behavioural strategy as everyone benefits; when I cooperate with you I also gain; when everyone cooperates everyone gains. This is a form of enlightened self-interest in which all the players in the game benefit through individuals avoiding taking too much. This applies to all aspects of social interaction, but it is also a central principle in environmental action, in which the game involves all humans and the banker is the environment. With enlightened restraint the environment will provide for the needs of humanity. Individuals who take too much, through over-consumption in its many forms, collectively add to environmental degradation.

In Indonesia there is a traditional way of catching monkeys which involves putting nuts in a bowl so that the monkey grabs hold of the nuts, but cannot withdraw the hand. As the monkey continues to hold on to the nuts it is eventually found by the trapper who takes it away for eating. We need collectively to realise that we need to let go of the peanuts; as Gandhi said 'the Earth has enough for everyone's need, but not everyone's greed'.

Approaches to environmental education

Environmental education is *about, in, through* and *for* the environment (DES 1990). The first two chapters have shown that, while science has contributed to the problems of the environment, science education can be harnessed to support all of these dimensions:

Learning about the environment: Scientific concepts developed for meaningful understanding of the world we live in will help provide a critical understanding of environmental issues to inform individual choices.

Learning in and through the environment: Experiences with a wide range of contexts in and out of the classroom will give meaningful experiences for children and help develop supportive attitudes to living things and the environment at large.

Learning for the environment: With developing understanding of the nature of environmental problems and choices, alongside positive caring and empathetic attitudes to other living things we create the possibility of informed motivation to support the environment. This is the ultimate aim of environmental education.

The following two case studies show how these elements can be drawn together to realise this aim in a way which is appropriate for primary children:

Case study 1: Drama based activities to enable a Year 3 group to explore a social context where care of the environment competes with the need for employment

This case study demonstrates that drama is a highly effective medium for motivating children and provides a meaningful context for learning (see Littledyke 1994b; 1998 for further classroom strategies and drama techniques). The drama structure was developed alongside classroom and environmental area activities based on a topic of 'Minibeasts'. This is shown in Figure 3.3.

The detailed development of this structure was negotiated with the children through the drama. However, the main purpose was to provide a social context where the children could experience some of the issues related to the tensions between protection of the environment and the need to provide jobs. The children were placed in role as villagers with high levels of unemployment, but with good environmental surroundings, which included a local pond and woodland with a rich variety of wildlife. A proposed building programme for a chemical factory and supermarket provided opportunity for employment, but change and possible deterioration in environmental quality. The drama was developed within this broad framework to enable the children in role to build up a narrative through their drama identities and interactions and to respond to the proposed changes, so creating opportunity to explore and understand the issues and dilemmas.

The children were predominantly in roles as villagers in families, with identities which they created, but it was also important to encourage them to consider fully the issues from all sides. Thus there were frequent time-out reflective discussion sessions where the significance of the implications of the action and choices of the villagers were discussed. The children were also put in different roles where they actively addressed different perspectives. For example, they were placed in role as petitioners persuading other local people to support the factory on the one hand, and following this they were placed in opposing roles petitioning against the factory. This ensured that all the arguments for and against were fully considered. At the council meeting, where the decision about the building proposals were made, each family carefully prepared a case to cover different aspects of the building programme. The issues of protection of the environment were prominent in their presentation, and the scientific understanding which developed from the classroom based activities informed their arguments. The children as villagers were largely against the proposals after considering the issues, though this was not the case in a similar structure developed elsewhere where the group was fairly evenly split (Littledyke 1989).

As follow-on to the decision about the building programme the children took on the roles of councillors who were making decisions about other planning proposals. These proposals included requests for fishing and fox hunting rights, a planned chicken farm and a proposed local zoo. Through these proposals the children were able to discuss the issues of use of animals for different purposes and to make recommendations in role about what they thought was appropriate. After much discussion and presentation of different points of view they finally agreed to grant fishing rights with the provisory that endangered species are not taken, while the fox-hunting rights were not granted because they considered it to be cruel to the foxes. The chicken farm had to be run on a free range system, which they considered provided the best conditions for the animals, while the zoo had to be run as a safari park with enough space and facilities for the animals. The discussions enabled the children to express different views and to hear the views of others. Kohlberg (1976) proposed that moral development can occur when children are exposed to higher stage moral reasoning, hence the drama forum created an opportunity for moral reasoning and moral development to occur as well as the use of scientific reasoning to support viewpoints.

This teaching programme was part of a research project funded by the Teacher Training Agency (see Littledyke *et al.* 1997c for the full report). Assessments of the children's learning were made and compared to a parallel control group which followed a similar classroom topic on Minibeasts but without the drama. The assessments showed that the children of the class who experienced the drama had far higher levels of interest and motivation in the classroom activities on the Minibeast topic (as well being highly engrossed in the drama), they showed better understanding of the science concepts which were being taught and they showed greater complexity of reasoning and articulation in justifying their views in interviews. We see a similar increased involvement whenever science is approached through issues requiring scientific understanding to debate them, as this next case study also shows.

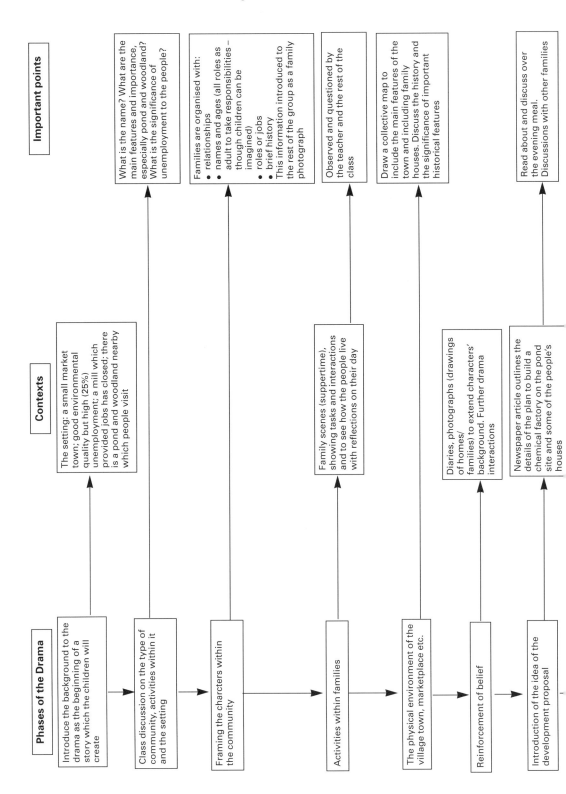

Phases of the Drama

Introduce the background to the drama as the beginning of a story which the children will create

Class discussion on the type of community, activities within it and the setting

Framing the characters within the community

Activities within families

The physical environment of the village town, marketplace etc.

Reinforcement of belief

Introduction of the idea of the development proposal

Contexts

The setting: a small market town; good environmental quality but high (25%) unemployment; a mill which provided jobs has closed; there is a pond and woodland nearby which people visit

Family scenes (suppertime), showing tasks and interactions and to see how the people live with reflections on their day

Diaries, photographs (drawings of homes/families) to extend characters' background. Further drama interactions

Newspaper article outlines the details of the plan to build a chemical factory on the pond site and some of the people's houses

Important points

What is the name? What are the main features and importance, especially pond and woodland? What is the significance of unemployment to the people?

Families are organised with:
- relationships
- names and ages (all roles as adult to take responsibilities – though children can be imagined)
- roles or jobs
- brief history
This information introduced to the rest of the group as a family photograph

Observed and questioned by the teacher and the rest of the class

Draw a collective map to include the main features of the town and including family houses. Discuss the history and the significance of important historical features

Read about and discuss over the evening meal. Discussions with other families

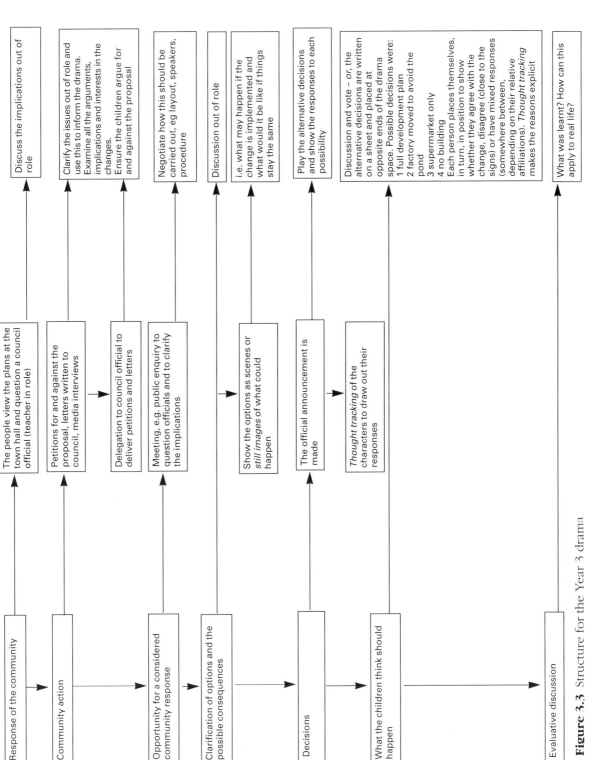

Figure 3.3 Structure for the Year 3 drama

Case study 2: 'Rubbish' topic with a Year 5 group

The topic commenced with a clean up (with due care for health and safety) of a path strewn with rubbish and adjacent to the school, which produced 20 full rubbish bags of waste! The rubbish was categorised into types of materials (metal, paper/cardboard/wood, glass, various plastics, organic) and pathways of the rubbish from their material origins in the Earth, through processing in factories, sale in shops, to disposal of the materials were researched, showing the different ways in which they were extracted from the Earth and used. The children visited a shop and a food factory; they asked questions about food processing and packaging and the children saw how the packaging was used. They made a survey of waste at home by estimating approximate volume of waste and the types of waste materials in each child's waste basket. The children questioned the local council about disposal policy and recycling activities and they saw slides of landfill sites and recycling centres. Cycles of production, use and waste which produce pollution were compared to non-polluting natural growth and decay cycles. This also showed how recycling processes were closer in procedure to natural cycles and emphasised to the children the need to prevent excessive waste (see Chapter 5 for more of the specific scientific ideas).

The children investigated properties of the materials and packages through scientific investigations for strength, durability, flexibility and suitability for stacking (or tessellation). They designed and made food packages as part of design and technology activities. Finally, a display of the activities was made and presented in a school assembly, by a static display in the local library and by creating a 'Rubbish Trail' on the local park with the children as 'Rubbish Guides' dressed up in a uniform constructed from rubbish bags and taking members of the public, including their parents, around their display of rubbish whilst explaining the issues. The maxim of the 3Rs: reduce, reuse, recycle to protect the environment was developed through this work and figured prominently in the final activities.

This topic produced high levels of interest and motivation with very high quality work from the children. The parents were also very impressed with their children's developing awareness of the issues.

Chapter 4

Faraday, bubbles and science processes

Liz Lakin

Chapters 2 and 3 explored the nature of science and its impact on the environment. In this chapter we explore the processes of science and how these relate to science education. To understand this we must ask such questions as:

- is being scientific a natural process and
- what *are* the processes of science?

We will answer these questions through examples from children's activities and show how science processes can be taught through the teaching environment. The chapter concludes with examples of good practice relating to the major environmental issues of the 21st century.

What is science?

'. . . look Miss, look! . . . I can put my finger through the bubble . . . and it's not burst!!' (Karen, 9 yrs)

This exclamation arose during a Science and Technology Week 99 activity entitled 'Bubbles and Slime'. Year 5 and Year 6 children (9–11 year olds) were exploring the properties of these common substances. They were acting as 'real scientists', observing, investigating, predicting and debating, but more importantly 'learning' from their actions and having 'fun' at the same time. This is 'science' in its purest sense; finding out about the world around us. As Harlen (1985, p. 4) explains 'science begins . . . when they (the children) realise that they can find things out for themselves by their own actions'.

During the 'Bubbles and Slime' activity, the children were being encouraged to challenge their own interpretations of what was happening in front of them using existing understanding and explanations, with help, guidance and 'expert scaffolding' from a few 'old-hands'. This is science education whereby children build an understanding of the world constructed from their own, often naive, interpretations which they challenge in the light of new experiences. Osborne and Freyberg (1985) see the aim of science education as enabling the learner to make better sense of the world around them by helping them reconstruct their ideas in a useful and meaningful manner. Driver *et al.* (1985) explain that even before encountering formal school science, children have constructed their own ideas of how the world works. These ideas have developed through personal experience with the physical world and through shared language and social understanding. These 'alternative conceptions' need to be elicited by the teacher, so that any necessary restructuring and future construction, can take place (see Chapter 1). It is the work of philosophers and scientists of the past, together with modern day advances and understanding that help provide the 'scaffolding' which supports the children's construction.

But how does science work?

Research by Edmondson and Novak (1993) suggests that children's views of how science works and is carried out, affects both the way they learn science and their attitude towards scientific knowledge. This being the case, it is important to elicit these views and images of what they think scientific work might be. Solomon *et al.* (1994) worked with 11–14 year olds exploring their ideas about how scientific knowledge is acquired. They classified the children's responses into seven images of scientists, most embodying some notion of how scientists go about getting to know the world. These ranged from the stereotypical cartoon image ('white-coated, wispy-haired, bespectacled male doing something reckless with a giant chemistry set'), through the vivisectionist, to the 'all-knowing' scientist as portrayed in television documentaries. They concluded that these ideas were a mixture of classroom experience and images gained from the wider community, but seldom from contact with a genuine scientist.

30 years ago, Ziman (1968) described science as '*public knowledge* . . . not merely *published knowledge* or information'. Anyone, he claims can make an observation, or conceive or put forward a hypothesis. Whether being scientific is natural and common to us all, or a craft accessible only to the gifted few or something that has to be learnt, is widely debated. In order to gain a feel for the debate, it is necessary to examine the so-called 'science process skills' which are fundamental to the argument:

- observing (notice something);
- hypothesing (form an idea to explain it);
- predicting;
- investigating (test the idea to see if it fits);
- debating (discuss the merits of the idea; how does it increase our understanding?).

Millar (1991) recognises these as general cognitive skills which all humans routinely employ from birth. But to what extent is scientific thinking natural? Matthews (1994) states that this is the most basic issue at stake in the evaluation of the constructivist approach to learning and teaching. He suggests that there is an under-riding assumption at the heart of constructivism that scientific thought is natural. He goes on to argue a fundamental flaw associated with this assumption:

> . . . science developed so late in human history, some 10,000 years after the development of agriculture, and 2,000 years after the intellectual achievements of the Greeks; and it developed in only one culture despite numerous cultures having advanced thought, literature, art, education and commerce. (1994, p. 161)

While Matthews's claim for science in 'one culture' is challenged by the existence of earlier Islamic science (Butt 1991), he makes the significant point that science is not natural and 'that scientific understanding and modes of thought require initiation into a scientific tradition, an initiation provided by school science teachers' (Matthews 1994, p. 161).

Brook *et al.* (1989) take the argument one stage further, claiming that scientific process skills, albeit generic cognitive skills, need to be honed and refined. Taking the example of 'observation', they explain that children don't necessarily see the 'patterns' the teacher intends them to see. How often do we hear a cry of exasperation as a child pulls her/his net from the pond or stream and empties it into the tray ? '*Oh, I've got nothing here!*' A few minutes of careful looking and the tray comes alive. Children, therefore, need to be taught to look selectively, from a scientific perspective. This is true for adults and children alike. Some Post Graduate Initial Teacher Training students were given a sample from the college pond, no instructions, just a selection of 'observing equipment', i.e. a binocular microscope; a range of viewers of varying magnification; some petri dishes and a spoon. Silence ensued for the first five minutes until somebody scooped up a damsel fly nymph and looked at it under the viewer. They were captivated '*Oh! look at this . . . watch it wriggle . . . look at its legs!*' and '*what are those things?*' pointing at its gills. A discussion then followed as to how this could be used in class with Key Stage 1 and 2 pupils. The greatest concern however, was being unable to identify the different organisms. It was emphasised that the important learning points, at this level, were not necessarily being able to name and identify every organism found in the school pond, but rather to be able to recognise differences and place them in categories with clearly defined criteria, for example:

- the number of legs;
- presence of a shell;
- ways of moving;
- number of appendages.

These categories imply that a concept of an animal already exists in the mind of observers and illustrate the interplay between sense data and these existing ideas: what you see, depends upon how you look at it! This was later enhanced by using a video camera, the 'flexicam', to display the sample on a television screen for the whole group to view.

In scientific terms, however, the above example was still only developing generic skills of observation and classifying, together with trying to stimulate inquiry. There is always the danger of only seeing what you expect/are expected to see. How many times has the unsuspecting student of biology painstakingly drawn an air-bubble at high power from a microscope slide, misinterpreting it for a cell. Then there were the 'A' Level students searching through beetroot cells for examples of plasmolysed cells – those which have shrunk as a result of desiccation. Having found examples they carefully drew them, only to discover that the sample was mistakenly from cooked beetroot and the cells were unable to respond to the varying saline solution they had been subjected to. What you see can depend upon what you expect to find!

It is becoming evident that *how* to observe and what patterns to look for needs to be taught at the same time as teaching about the models and ideas of science: children need to have a purpose in their observations and to know why they are looking. It is purposeful observation that helps scientists interpret their observations, make predictions and draw conclusions. Millar (1991) sees these processes as being inseparable. They are held together by the way scientists work, developing and evaluating their ideas. There are no set rules that govern how these processes are carried out, nor indeed how scientific methods develop. It does, however involve the use of certain skills, for example:

- after noticing something that catches attention, deciding to observe;
- deciding what to focus on and what to ignore, giving a purpose to observation;
- making predictions from ideas and deciding whether they are fulfilled;
- interpreting and drawing inferences;
- drawing conclusions.

These cannot be taught, nor are they written in 'tablets of stone' to be commissioned when required. Much of a scientist's knowledge of what to do is tacit – it is implied or understood without being stated. To this end, a scientist is practising a craft. Millar (1994) sees this as the 'art of doing science', something, he claims that good science teachers emphasise and that *all* teachers of science should be encouraged to do. This has implications for the way science is taught in the classroom, away from the 'discovery learning' approach, modelled on an inductive view of science which leads to teachers '. . . spending an ever increasing share of classroom time on making 'process-based' assessments of doubtful validity' (Millar 1994, p. 175).

Millar goes on to point out that science has to have characteristic ways of working and characteristic standards of judgements to ensure that theories and 'facts' can stand the test of time, surviving critical study and testing by others. These are governed by the 'current conceptions in the field of study as well as by available technologies and are influenced by the purposes for which the inquiry is undertaken' (Millar 1994, p. 174). Furthermore, scientific ideas are never true in an absolute sense as ideas are subject to revision in the light of new evidence (Popper 1963). When we consider this approach, we can begin to understand the provisional nature of science.

Understanding science

To develop this further, it is necessary to gain an appreciation of how science and the scientific community works. As discussed in Chapter 2, too often science is seen as:

- objective;
- capable of yielding ultimate truths;
- proving things;
- having a defined and unique subject matter;
- having unique methods;
- being value free.

Ross dismisses this approach and urges us to consider how scientific theory has developed in the past. He explains that the history of science is 'punctuated by revolutions in thought as one idea is replaced by another' (1998, p. 78).

By exploring the historical developments within science, we can begin to form a more realistic view and understanding of how science works. Solomon *et al.* (1994) suggest that stories of actual activities of scientists are memorable enough to put across new ideas about the nature of scientific knowledge to young pupils. Take for example, electricity generation. For decades scientists had battled with this '*amber fluid*', making irregular developments in unravelling its mysteries. The story involves a range of characters from very different backgrounds, all investigating, unbeknown to themselves, the same phenomenon. Their commonality was the drive to make sense of the world around them.

600 BC	Thales, a Greek, found that when amber was rubbed with silk it attracted feathers and other light objects – 'static electricity' had been discovered (electron = Greek for amber).
1752	The scene opens with Benjamin Franklin flying his kite in a thunder storm – 'positive and negative electricity' is introduced.
1800	Galvani's famous discovery with frogs' legs! By passing an electric current through the muscle tissue he managed to get the legs to twitch. Alessandro Volta developed this idea and created the first simple cells using pure silver and zinc discs sandwiched between muslin soaked in a salt solution.
1820	The connection between electricity and magnetism was discovered by Hans Christian Oersted, who demonstrated the effect a conductor carrying an electric charge had on the needle of a compass.
1820	Dominique-Francois Arago discovered the magnetic effect of electricity passing through a copper wire; reiterating the relationship between electricity and magnetism.
1821	Thomas John Seebeck found that by heating the junction of different metals, electricity was produced. Thermo-electricity had been discovered.
1830	Charles Wheatstone experiments with temperature difference in the same material, demonstrating that this difference in potential was

sufficient for electricity to flow. He perceived this as a future large scale
generation process.

1831   Michael Faraday recognises that the 'amber fluid' his fellow scientists had
been investigating was one and the same thing; electricity. He carried
out a series of experiments demonstrating electromagnetic induction and
introduced the means for generation on a commercial scale that is still
used today.

When we explore the biographical details of some of the characters, the
serendipitous nature of science shines through:

Charles Wheatstone, born in Gloucester in the early 1800s, was introduced to
electricity by reading about Volta's experiments, in French. With the help of his
brother he repeated several of these experiments in the kitchen of his father's
house, using a home-made battery. From these early beginnings came a life as
interesting as his mind was inquiring. For Wheatstone the questions 'why?',
'how?' and 'what if?' led to a world of discovery and intrigue.

Michael Faraday, born the son of a blacksmith, discovered for himself the
wonder of science through the books he read and the many experiments and
investigations he tried, using whatever equipment he could get or make. He
recognised the provisional nature of science, rejecting earlier theories and
revolutionising the 19th century understanding of the world. He studied the
work of his fellow scientists alongside his own investigations. He saw 'patterns'
and recognised similarities, enabling him to make the breakthroughs he did. He
recognised the need for a public understanding of science and introduced the
much acclaimed 'Royal Institution Christmas Lectures', which continue today.
Faraday realised how important it was for people to know how scientific ideas
developed and were evaluated. Applying this philosophy to our teaching of
science, teachers will need to know something about the body of knowledge
they are teaching, something about how this knowledge has come together, how
its claims are justified and what its limitations are, thereby enabling pupils to
appreciate the significance of sharing and revising ideas, and gain confidence in
trying and testing their own ideas (Borgford 1992).

Developing our understanding of science

Science, therefore, goes beyond merely observing and describing events and
phenomena in the natural world. It involves creating ideas and models, and an
element of 'cognitive conflict' – to pause, wonder and think again (CASE 1999, p.
2). Put in terms of the Piagetian model of cognitive development, thinking
science is all about encouraging the development of thinking from the concrete
operational stage to the formal operational stage (see Table 4.1).

Concrete operational	coping with limited variables; being able to describe rather than explain
	Level 3/4 National Curriculum assessment levels
Formal operational	can handle multi-variable patterns and can explain
	Level 5/6 upwards
	CASE (1992)

Table 4.1 Piaget's stages of cognitive development

This model immediately seems to preclude the learning of science for the early years pupils and indeed some of the later years. However, this is definitely not the case. Woolnough (1991) describes a model of learning in science which emphasises individual growth, starting from the very young and progressing upwards. He advocates that a science course should contain the following affective aspects:

- Play – Practical Experiences to build a feel for the phenomena and an interest in the area.
- Practice – Practical Exercises to develop competence in specific skills and techniques.
- Exploring – Practical Investigations to acquire stimulation, confidence and the ability to work as a problem-solving scientist.

Woolnough emphasises that the pupil needs '. . . to be given freedom to play, to practise and explore . . .' (p. 187). He sees the teacher's main tasks as creating the space, sustaining dialogue and introducing structures, problems and evaluations. In these days of literacy and numeracy dominance, we need to recognise the value of science at Key Stage 1. Children develop their own ideas about the world around them from birth and possibly before, and these ideas form the foundations of future scientific development.

Johnstone (1998) explains how children learn about gravity and forces from an early age. As they throw a toy out of their pram or high chair, it becomes a game – they look *down* for the lost toy and await someone picking up. This informal scientific knowledge is developed through informal experiences, then nurtured into an understanding of the world through formal learning situations. Much of the exploration is done through play at this age. Its role should not, however, be underestimated. Browne *et al.* (1997) see teacher intervention as having a crucial part to play during these early discovery sessions. The teacher may draw attention to what the child is doing, ask for comparisons and evaluations to be made, seek ideas from the children and ask for advantageous alternatives. This time for discussion and reflection enables the child to construct, re-visit and, if necessary, restructure their understanding. Science is viewed here as a method of inquiry as well as the rudiments of conceptual development, the latter being synonymous with the former.

This final point was brought home to an advisory teacher early on in his career. He recalls how a group of children helped him to sort out the real nature of a scientific test. Pattinson (1998) explains how he was invited into a Year 4 class to do some investigative work on melting. Armed with his cooler box and ice lollies he set the class the task of ensuring that their ice lolly could get back to their part of the beach without melting. The activity started and he went from group to group discussing with the children what they were doing. Was it a fair test and what were they measuring? He describes how, after some probing he got the answers he was looking for, until he visited the final group. The reply came: '*We are testing our idea to see how good it is*'. This floored him initially until he realised that that indeed was what the activity was all about; the procedures were merely a way of achieving it! To summarise the approach:

> By helping children through their own revolutions in thought and preparing them for more to come, we can begin to show children the nature of science: not a set of principles, but our continuing and imaginative attempts to create mental models of our environment which we can use to help us explore ever more deeply, with our senses and sensors. (Ross 1998, p. 78)

Achieving this constructive approach in the classroom

Context

Having analysed the nature of science and discussed its role and importance in developing an understanding of science, how can we ensure that such under-standing is achieved in the learning environment? Kirkham (1989) advocates that a balanced science education will involve an equilibrium between process, content and context, seeing the latter as relating science education to the individual, society and to the whole curriculum. He continues by stating that 'many children have a poor experience of science because it appears to invite little personal involvement, to be abstract and unrelated to real life' (Kirkham 1989, p. 148). This view is supported by Qualter (1996) who sees science as being accessible to all, not merely in that all children *do* science in the classroom but in that the science they do is relevant to them, and that it addresses issues pertinent to them.

The value of this was highlighted in a 'Science and Environment Day' conducted by a Gloucestershire Primary School. Years 5 and 6 pupils had been studying the Common adjacent to their school. Owned by the Commoners it is used by grazing birds, especially a flock of Bewick swans. These have given the Common its English Heritage title and Site of Special Scientific Interest (SSSI) status. Controversy abides over the future of the Common because it is drying out, owing to excessive drainage. The local fish smokery wants to flood the site and use it for fish stocks. Neighbouring farmers want it drained so that it can be turned over to farming. The pupils had visited the smokery and researched the history of the site, but they needed to visit the Common and find out what it was and what lived there.

Groups of pupils explored the floral ecology of the site; others investigated the ancient hedgerows around the periphery. Water samples from the rhines and soil samples from the meadows were taken and analysed back at school. The session concluded with rhine dipping, which revealed a host of exciting creatures ranging from nymphs to elvers. Back at school the samples' analysis revealed an interesting story, with the children watching it unfold as they added their data to the results table. Nitrate and phosphate levels in the water seemed surprisingly high. The rhine biodiversity and results from the remaining chemical analysis suggested that this excess was a recent introduction. This was explained to the pupils but one boy could be seen mulling it all over in his mind. He asked what phosphates did and it became clear that he had come across the term before. His questions continued, then he exclaimed that the phosphates could have come from the use of artificial fertiliser. His father was a farmer and the boy recognised the term 'phosphate' from discussions at home. It was then necessary to emphasise to the pupils that the samples they had taken were from a 'window' in the life of the Common. Discussions ensued as to whether or not the results were reliable and what would have to be done to ensure that they were getting a true indication of what was happening on the Common.

On that one day the pupils learnt a great deal about their environment; how it worked and how vulnerable it can be. They were introduced to several new techniques and developed new skills. Their scientific understanding of the inter-relatedness of the components of that ecosystem was developed and they began to draw conclusions express concerns and take actions about their environment. They had been acting like scientists. There were no discipline problems during the day; no lack of motivation or boredom, the real challenge came when the school buses arrived – the pupils didn't want to leave.

To ensure continuity and reduce the risk of science being held in isolation from other curriculum subject areas, the class teacher continued the theme of the 'Common' over the next few days, drawing on experiences and skills learnt. She was able to use the data gathered for maths sessions and the children recorded the event as part of their 'creative writing' lesson. Making the curriculum relevant and, at the same time, giving the children ownership of the content, led to a more in-depth understanding of the subject and contributed to their individual conceptual development.

Bubbles

In the example outlined above, the children were given the opportunity to develop new skills and techniques, while also developing an interest in and a feel for, being scientific. The more creative aspect of science described earlier in this chapter, requires challenges and exploration to allow it to blossom. Ravertz (1971, cited in Woolnough 1991, p. 46) describes scientific work as a 'craft activity, depending on a personal knowledge of particular things and a subtle judgement of their property'. This became evident during a science session with Years 5 and 6 pupils exploring bubbles. They were challenged to blow a bubble inside a bubble, to make a three bubble, then a six bubble dome and then to make a square bubble. Bubbles are something that children have played with from an early age, yet they are not always familiar with them as a science resource. Just to be able to blow a bubble from a film of soapy suds caught on the top of a plastic cup, caused enough problems.

> The child knows that inserting the straw into the bubble will cause it to burst – yet, '*He can blow it up!*' exclaims the exasperated child, looking over at a neighbour. The child tries again but this time the straw is damp with suds from the previous attempts – it goes through! Now to blow it up – '*pop!*' '*The bubble's burst!*' she cries disbelievingly.

It is a learning experience all the way, yet the activity is something so familiar; they've done it before; making bubbles in the bath; blowing hundreds in the garden, so why not now? The child soon realises that she has to blow gently. Eventually she can blow bubbles within bubbles. With this skill achieved, when challenged to put her finger through the bubble, it is a short step to transfer the knowledge gained and apply it to this new situation. Eagerly smoothing her finger in soapy suds, she proudly pokes it through the bubble. '*Look Miss, look! I can put my finger through the bubble . . . and it's not burst!!*' (Karen, nine years)

The children soon appreciate the significance of the suds when the bubble bursts, because it has touched a dry part of finger. The learning is there, but so too is the fun. One child even used a pair of scissors in the same way exclaiming '*Look! I can cut my bubble!*'.

During these sessions the children learnt about surface tension, experiencing the 'pull' of the bubble film on their fingers as they moved them into and out of bubbles; they experienced tessellation and how bubbles form on each other; how the colours of the rainbow form on the bubble's surface and swirl in the film. They made creative bubble creatures and giant bubbles with hoops which they could shake hands through, but they also learnt what was so special about soapy suds and why they were necessary to make bubbles.

It's not just the children who learn from such experiences, their teachers were enthralled. They took up the challenge and explained that they hadn't had so much fun for ages and felt that they learnt so much!

Content

Having recognised the need to relate science to everyday life and to set it in a 'real context', we can begin to appreciate that through the consideration and evaluation of 'alternative concepts', children's ideas and models develop and change while still continuing to 'make sense' in terms of their experience. This may take time but it is necessary if we are to avoid children seeing school science as a form of fantasy and distinct from their everyday lives. This is enhanced by ensuring that:

- The 'content' of the science session is 'knowable' by the children; that it will be of some use to them and not merely the next isolated topic, totally alien to anything outside of the science lesson.

Science content encompasses the facts, symbols and terminology as well as concepts, ideas and models of science. Context is crucial, for instance, in the

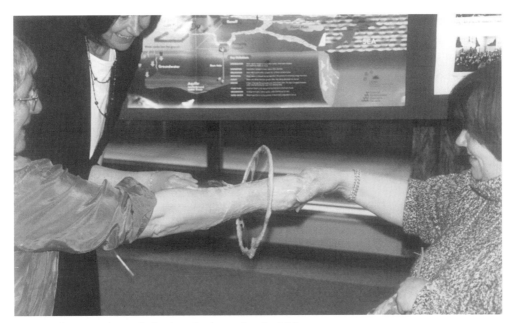

Figure 4.1 Teachers shake hands through a bubble

previous instance, of the pupils in Gloucestershire exploring the Common, they were encouraged to handle the ideas and make them their own. The content of the activity became 'knowable' through their own involvement. This led to a greater appreciation of the natural and artificial environment, increasing the children's appreciation and enjoyment of it.

- When learning about different concepts, application and usefulness needs to be emphasised.

A Year 7 child was struggling with isosceles triangles as part of a geometry homework. '*When am I ever going to use these?*' she cried, totally bewildered and fed up! A month or so later, while on a sailing holiday she looks over her Dad's shoulder whilst he's plotting the day's course. '*Hey, that's an isosceles triangle!*' '*Yes,*' says her Dad '*I use them to plot running fixes and work out the route home*'.

- The content should contain some scientific knowledge about the major issues in our society such as environmental pollution, the energy scene, national and global resources.

One of the most effective strategies for developing an understanding of such controversial issues is through role play exercises, decision making scenarios and peer group presentations. Millar and Osborne (1998) recommend this approach in their review of the current National Curriculum for Science. When conducting this in class, the following aims and ground rules should be born in mind:

- ensure pupils gain a systematic exposure to the issues at stake and a sufficiently balanced consideration of the range of views held;

- pupils must be encouraged to appreciate the points of view held by others;
- pupils are entitled to experiment safely with their own thoughts about the matter being considered;
- appropriate boundaries made must be made clear to indicate what, if any, are unacceptable behaviours.

These have been brought together in an initiative pioneered by a national electricity generation company, as described below.

The Energy Game

The Energy Game, suitable for older Key Stage 2 pupils, is a decision making exercise which involves pupils in exploring the controversial issues associated with satisfying the ever increasing demand for electrical energy. With several clearly defined objectives, the game introduces pupils to the generation of electrical energy and associated energy sources. Consideration has to be given to the environmental, social and economic impacts of generation from a variety of energy sources, while respecting the views of others. The plethora of information available requires that pupils practice and develop research skills as well as developing collaborative team work. On completion of their decision making exercise, pupils present their findings to their peers using over-head transparencies, thus developing presentation skills.

In contrast with many other classroom situations, pupils are encouraged to talk and debate. The noise level reveals a great deal: too quiet and the pupils are having difficulties, too noisy and they are shouting and arguing with each other. The facilitator during the game will intervene when necessary, correcting any misconceptions and monitoring proceedings. Throughout the 'game' children develop personal abilities and attitudes such as confidence, perseverance and initiative, which will need to be nurtured and enhanced in order to be taken with them into other aspects of their learning.

Finally

- Content should enable pupils to understand the provisional nature of science, that science knowledge has its limitations and is not the only form of 'useful' knowledge. A balanced approach should be developed that compares and contrasts other forms of knowledge.

This has rarely been more true than when we consider one of the major scientific and environmental issues of the past decade, that of genetic modification (GM) of food. Seldom does a week pass without some mention of genetics and genetic modification in the press. A recent breakthrough involves the discovery and isolation of the gene controlling height in crops such as wheat. Its significance is such that when transplanted into rice it produces a dwarf variety. Dwarfness in crop plants is invariably associated with high yields because of stronger stems.

Scientific and technological advances with implications for future food supplies and public health, while at the same time being potential 'money-spinners', tend to spark people's interests and emotions.

In the height of the GM food crisis in 1999, when 'potatoes' had over-taken 'tomatoes' as being the 'in-crop' to modify genetically, Professor Pennington (a governor of Rowett Research Institute, Aberdeen, where Dr. Arpad Pusztai carried out his research into genetic manipulation of potatoes) described what began as an investigation into the science behind Dr. Pusztai's claims, as a 'fully fledged food scare'. Pennington explains that 'the GM food debate . . . highlights some general principles which are not at all as well understood as they should be. These are the nature of the scientific method, the limits that attend the role of scientists in policy making, and the way that the media works' (Pennington 1999, p. 51).

Pennington likens the role of the media to a Gregorian telescope, capturing, reflecting and magnifying a story, claiming that its (the media's) eye focuses particularly on issues like alleged 'cover-ups', 'human interest' stories, conflicts and questions of blame. All of which is subsumed within the GM debate; so why let the facts stand in the way of a good story! The media portray scientists as 'supreme "knowers" with any discrepancies between the scientific "experts" as evidence of bias or incompetence' (Millar 1994, p. 173). This view is supported by Edmondson and Novak (1993) who, after systematic analysis of the content of scientific news stories, scientific journalism and magazine features, conclude that such stories contain limited explanation but are strong on scientific authority. This makes it all the more important to understand that the nature of science as debate is at the core of good science; the significant point is to be able to weigh up evidence and arguments to assess the validity of any particular view, rather than make an assumption that one scientist holds the firm truth while another must by definition be wrong.

Children of today are the decision makers of tomorrow. They require a firm and knowledgeable basis on which to make those decisions. They need to consider new technologies and their products on their merits; weighing benefits against risks and coming to a rational conclusion, based on science and other forms of knowledge, not sentiment.

Summary

The fundamental aims of science education need to be made clear: to develop 'well-rounded individuals, excited and curious about the world around them, not afraid to question their ideas and the ideas of others . . . who can see the value of scientific skills and conceptual understanding in their everyday lives' (Johnstone 1998, p. 81). To achieve this we need to ensure that all scientific experiences are positive learning experiences for children whatever their age.

In the early years of development, play provides the vehicle for practical experiences; getting a feel for and developing an interest in, science and the world around us. This will be interspersed with opportunities to practise and refine skills and competencies. Exploration and investigation will serve to stimulate inquiry, developing the child's confidence and scientific skills. The proportions of play, practice and exploration will vary progressively at different ages and stages of development. There is however a strong argument to maintain all three facets in science teaching, to ensure individual conceptual growth within the art of 'doing science'.

Chapter 5

Matter and life – the cycling of materials

Keith Ross

This chapter examines the fate of materials discarded by us into the environment. For this we need to establish the range of materials that occur around us and their composition. We then need to examine the way they might interfere with living things.

Fundamental to all this is the concept of the atom – the indestructible building block of all matter. Although materials are changing all the time, the atoms from which they are made up remain unchanged. If we understand how living things function at an atomic level we can begin to grasp why some materials are toxic or harmful whereas others are benign or even beneficial to life. We begin to see planet Earth working as a series of cycles from the simplicity of the water cycle through to the most complex cycling of materials by the processes of life itself. In all these processes materials, at an atomic level, are transported but never generated or used up. We used this concept to illustrate a constructivist approach to learning in Chapter 1.

In the primary school these ideas are best approached by getting children to think about where materials come from (for example, a wooden table, a china plate, a metal spoon, a bowl of cereal). This process of tracing things back shows that materials always come from somewhere – in the same way they don't disappear when they are eaten or thrown away. (See Case study 2 'Rubbish topic with a Year 5 group' in Chapter 3.)

This chapter begins with an examination of the materials present on Earth. We then look at the great cycles which transform and transport them. Finally we compare the workings of life with our throw-away culture, and show what can be done to develop a sustainable lifestyle for mankind.

What substances make up our environment?

People have tried to make sense of the millions of different substances around them – the Greeks suggested that all matter was made of the four elements (earth, water, air and fire – suggestive of solids, liquids, gases and energy?). The

Islamic school (AD 750–1350) (Butt 1991) used experimentation to realise that some materials, such as mercury and sulphur, appeared to be 'elemental' and made up of only themselves, whereas other materials seem to be compounded. The alchemists (pre-Renaissance Europe) recognised elements, but hoped they could be transformed to gold. Dalton's atomic theory (AD 1810) made sense of the growing concept of unchangeable elements, and Mendeleev (AD 1865) developed his periodic table to classify and make sense of the hundred elements that make up all materials around us.

Even though elements can be classified according to their position on the periodic table, very few substances around us are elements. How can we begin to make sense of these millions of different compounds? The system we describe here, called 'The structure triangle' (Ross 1997), may seem to many an over-simplification, but it has the advantage that you arrive at the same system whether you start from observable properties of the substances, or from a consideration of type of elements from which they are made. It reduces the millions of substances to just five basic structures.

A useful task is to try to match the following ten substances into five pairs, according to their structural and physical properties.

leather	candle wax	wood-ash	concrete	nylon
baking soda	copper	granite	steel	air

We need to ask:

When you hit it with hammer does it: return to its original shape; stay bent or becomes dented; shatter . . .?

When it is heated: does it melt or boil easily (or is it already a gas?); does it char then catch fire; or does it just get hot?

Does it conduct electricity as a solid? when molten or in solution in water? not at all?

Does it dissolve in water; in petrol; in lava; in molten iron . . .?

People often start by classifying substances as manufactured or natural: thus leather and nylon (which are chemically and physically very similar) are put into different groups. In the same way concrete and granite are often classified into different groups. Here are the five groups which comprise the structure triangle

- **Metals** (copper and steel) bend, conduct heat and electricity, are crystalline and have high boiling points. Metals 'dissolve' other metals, forming alloys such as brass, solder, and tooth amalgam. Other substances, however, do not dissolve in molten metals (the slag in iron-making floats, the sand used to cast metals does not dissolve during casting).

- **Rocks** (granite and concrete) are brittle, have high melting and boiling points. Note that they do eventually melt (seen as lava in volcanoes), and that when molten they all seem to dissolve to form a single liquid, from which a variety of crystals form when the lava solidifies. These crystals are easily seen in granite, a very common igneous rock (= formed from molten rock, as in the word *ignite*, from Greek igni = fire) with large crystals.

- **Life-polymers** (nylon and leather) are tough but flexible and are fibrous. They are materials made from carbon, either directly by life processes, or manufactured from fossil fuels, themselves the product of material that was once living. Note that those made directly by living things (natural fibres/polymers like wood, hair and silk) are biodegradable unlike those manufactured from petroleum (man-made fibres and plastics). Apart from this important distinction, all these 'life polymers' behave in a very similar way.

  If life polymers are heated in a closed space they simply decompose (char-burn), and remain fuels. This happens to all organic matter trapped in sediment and squeezed and heated over geological time to form fossil fuels, and it also happens in our gut, where digestion cuts the long polymers of our food into bits small enough to enter our blood where most are used as fuel. The faeces which remain 'un-cut', and some unwanted gases also make good fuels.

  If life polymers are heated in open air they all catch fire and flame-burn, forming carbon dioxide and water vapour (exactly the same happens to biodegradable materials when they are used as a fuel in the bodies of decay-causing animals during the process of respiration). Note that when burnt in air natural organic polymers will leave a small amount of whitish ash (metal oxides, evidence of the minerals taken up from the soil by plants), whereas manufactured plastics often leave no ash when they combust.

- **Volatile materials** (candle wax and air) have little or no strength, dissolve in other volatile substances, and are easily vaporised or are already gases at room temperature. If you are confused by solid wax and gaseous air both being classified in a single group, remember that all materials (unless they decompose) can exist in solid, liquid and gaseous forms, depending on temperature (and pressure). Volatile materials are simply those that turn to gases at relatively low temperatures. They are composed of small molecules that do not attract each other strongly, which accounts for their low boiling point and lack of physical strength.

- **Ionic materials** (baking soda and wood-ash) are brittle, crystalline, dissolve in water, they only conduct electricity (and decompose as they do so) when molten or dissolved, and have high melting and boiling points. If you are confused by wood-ash, remember that it is a grey powder which is used as a fertiliser – it contains the mineral salts needed by plants which dissolve in the rain and enter the roots, and are left behind again when the plant burns. This is perhaps the least familiar of all the categories. Note how different **sugar** (volatile) is from **salt** (ionic): there is no change when salt is heated, unless very high temperatures are reached, in which case salt melts and is then able to conduct electricity. Sugar, of course, melts, then tends to char when heated – it never conducts electricity.

This five substance classification is more helpful than solid, liquid and gas, because, as noted above, all substances can exist in solid, liquid and gaseous forms. We use each of these five substance types for different purposes which depend on their properties. Thus copper (metal: ductile and conducting) is used for electrical wires. Bricks (rock: hard and brittle) are used for house walls. Nylon (life polymer: tough and flexible) is used for clothes. The other two types are not usually used for making things because they either have too little strength (volatile: wax) or they dissolve in water (ionic: salts). Instead they are used for their chemical properties, e.g. fragrant oils (volatile) are used by plants to attract pollinators, and minerals in the soils (ionic salts) are used by plants for growth.

Think about any substance, and you will be able to place it in one of these five categories. The next section looks at the atomic make-up of them, and we shall see the same five structure types emerging from the way different atoms bond together.

Unchanging atoms amidst change

At the heart of an understanding of materials is the idea that they are made only from atoms which can rearrange themselves but cannot be destroyed (except in nuclear processes). The important idea here is that the atoms within matter do not change when the material itself changes, they simply join up in a different way. The Lego analogy is a good one – when you convert a Lego garage into a Lego house, the bricks (building blocks or atoms) remain unchanged, they just join in a different way. See Chapter 1 for a discussion on teaching approaches.

There are only about 100 different atoms, represented by the elements of the periodic table, of which about 25 make up the bulk of what we see around us. Many children leave school 'knowing' that matter is made of particles, but believing that these particles are just little bits of sugar, iron, plastic etc. They think that the 'atoms' melt, burn, expand, dissolve, just like the real materials do. One of the biggest barriers preventing people from understanding the world from a chemical point of view is the problem of seeing atoms as unchanging amid change. Melting is when particles, previously in fixed positions, are able to slide past each other; burning is where oxygen atoms from the air join with the atoms in the fuel . . . and so on.

Another barrier to understanding is the naïve idea that gases are not made of matter whereas in fact all liquids and gases will become solid if cooled to a low enough temperature, and all solids and liquids will turn to gases when heated strongly enough, though some will decompose before this. Thus air can be liquefied (at very low temperatures), and so can rocks (at very high temperatures). Matter seems to disappear in many processes such as evaporation and burning. It is only through an understanding of the material nature of gases that these processes can be understood in terms of the indestructibility of particles.

The structure triangle

A study of theories of chemical bonding allows us to account, theoretically, for the five categories established above (Ross and Lakin 1996, 1998; Ross 1997). For those with an interest in chemistry this brief section outlines this story. When Dalton published his notion of atoms in 1810 less than half of the elements were known. But the idea was a powerful one – an element was a special form of matter which was made of only one type of particle – an oxygen atom for oxygen, a sulphur atom for sulphur, etc. All other materials were compounds made of two or more different elements.

Many people tried to make sense of the different elements but it was not until 1869 that the periodic table was 'invented' by Mendeleev. It was only by leaving gaps (for elements yet to be discovered) that he was able to show clear patterns in reactivity of the chemical elements.

The periodic table has a simple structure: if elements are arranged in a line according to the weight of their atoms, their properties (such as the element's boiling point, or chemical reactivity) repeat themselves in cycles or 'periods'. The table is then constructed so that the elements that behaved in a similar way were placed beneath each other, but they are still kept in order of increasing atomic weight.

Later the development of our understanding of the electronic structure of atoms, as composed of a nucleus and 'orbiting' electrons, provided a theoretical base for these patterns. Bonding between atoms depends on the arrangement of the electrons on the outside of atoms. These outer electrons help to 'glue' atoms together, and this explains why elements in the same group behave in the same way – they all have identical outer shells of electrons (e.g. carbon, silicon, germanium in group 4 all have 4 outer electrons). However, there is a gradual increase in non-metallic behaviour as we go *up* a group or *across* a period, allowing us to place all the elements in order from the most reactive metal (like sodium) to the most reactive non-metal (like chlorine). If this line of elements is flattened, it forms the top of what is called the *structure triangle*. (Figure 5.1) (Ross 1997).

If you react sodium with chlorine you get a compound that is totally unlike the constituents (common salt – sodium chloride in this example). We now construct a triangle by drawing lines from these extremely reactive elements to meet at the apex which represents the salt (see Figure 5.1). All other compounds (of two elements) can now be located within the triangle at the place where similar lines from the two elements meet with the elements themselves along the top line. The five structures we started with are formed from the five possible combinations of atoms: metal with metal (**metals**), non-metal with non-metal (**volatile**), the in-between elements bonding with themselves (Silicon forming 3D giant **rock**-like structures, and Carbon forming giant linear polymers to produce **life-polymers**), and finally metal with non-metal (**ionic**). No other structures are possible.

The validity of this scheme for classifying substances is that we get the same five structures whether we start from the real materials in the common

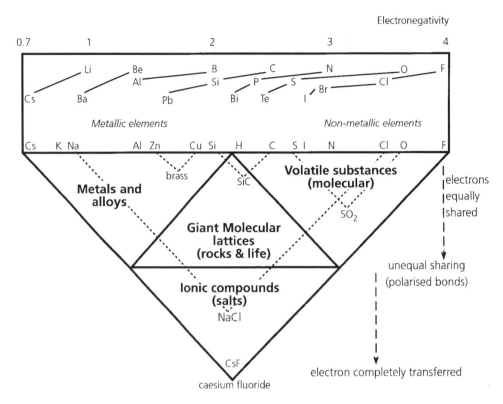

Figure 5.1 The structure triangle

experience of pupils, or consider the elemental make up of the substances, and the nature of the forces that hold, or fail to hold, their atoms together.

With this understanding of the structure of the materials in our environment we can now look at the way they are cycled naturally, and then consider what happens when humans start to interfere with these natural cycles.

Recently humans have not re-cycled the material they use. Consequently we have begun to run out of new resources and also run out of places to dump waste. Thus a resource and pollution crisis has developed which endangers many ecosystems and threatens to change the global climate. To understand the possible problems caused by materials discarded by humans into the environment, we need to understand how these natural cycles work.

Three great cycles of nature

Materials get cycled in nature in three main ways:

climate (meteorology)
rocks (geology)
life (biology)

Climate (meteorology)

Volatile materials, from our chimneys, exhaust pipes and aerosol cans end up in the atmosphere. To understand how they can upset material cycles and energy flows requires an understanding of the nature of gases (i.e. of the atmosphere) and how they are held to the Earth by gravity. We then need to establish the nature of the radiation coming to us from the sun, the source of almost all the energy needed to keep the materials of climate, life and rocks cycling.

Television pictures of the US moon missions help to focus our ideas about the nature of gravity. It is interesting to compare Newton's (AD 1642 to 1727) revolutionary ideas of motion and gravity with those of the Greek philosopher, Aristotle, (348–322 BC) which were much like those of children and non-scientific adults today. Aristotle thought that the natural state of water and earth was to fall downwards (to Earth), and that of fire and air was to rise (to the heavens). Newton proposed a universal force of attraction, which he called gravity, acting between any two bodies.

The problem Aristotle had with air is a problem we all have to deal with: air appears to be weightless, and sometimes it does rise (e.g. when it is hot). Yet air is made of atoms, which have mass, so our atmosphere itself is 'heavy' and is attracted to the Earth by gravity. If you pump air into a football the ball gets heavier, just as SCUBA divers' air bottles get lighter as the air is used. To understand the structure of the lower parts of the atmosphere we need to look next at the incoming and outgoing radiant energy.

The electromagnetic spectrum, from low energy radio waves, through visible light to high energy x-rays, will be familiar to most of you (see Figure 5.2). All electromagnetic radiation (emr) travels through a vacuum at the speed of light.

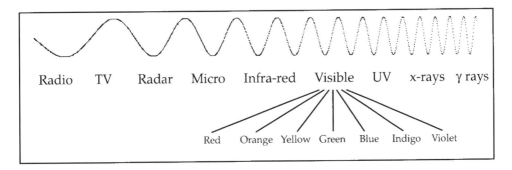

Figure 5.2 The electromagnetic spectrum

The energy we get from the sun is mainly visible light that goes straight through the atmosphere and heats the earth's surface. The sun's ultra violet light (UV) is stopped by ozone in the upper atmosphere, so very little reaches the surface. This means that the atmosphere is heated from below (from visible light heating the ground) and above (from UV absorbed by ozone), with the coldest part sandwiched in between. Below this cold tropopause we have hot air developing underneath cold. The denser colder air sinks, forcing the hot air up (this is why hot air, despite its weight, tends to rise against gravity). The turbulence so caused gives us our weather – and this lowest region containing most of the air, the troposphere, is thus often called the weather zone. Above this there is a calm, stable layer called the stratosphere where the hot air, heated by UV, sits above cold, where jet aeroplanes fly above the weather and clouds.

The ozone 'layer' and CFCs (stratosphere)

Although energy reaches us from the sun mainly as visible light, this is accompanied by the more dangerous higher energy ultraviolet (UV) light. UV has enough energy to break molecules apart causing chemical damage. Ozone formation is a continuous process in which oxygen molecules (O_2, or di-oxygen) in the upper atmosphere (stratosphere) are split by UV into separate atoms. These single atoms bond with di-oxygen to form ozone (O_3, or tri-oxygen). So ozone is created from oxygen by UV light from the sun. The O_3 thus created absorbs UV far better than the original oxygen, splitting back to an oxygen atom and molecule as it does so, in a regenerating cycle. This prevents UV from reaching the Earth's surface where it could do the same sort of chemical damage but to biological molecules, especially DNA, resulting in mutations, cell death or cancers. (Note that ozone is also formed in the troposphere as a result of motor car exhausts. Here it is a pollutant, helping to accentuate acid rain.)

Chloro-fluoro-carbons (CFCs) are small molecules made of carbon, chlorine and fluorine atoms. They are extremely stable molecules, harmless to living things and are used as refrigerant fluids, as industrial solvents and to 'blow' insulation materials such as expanded polystyrene. It is ironic that CFCs, so benign in the troposphere become so destructive once they move up into the stratosphere. Most volatile pollutants are soluble in rain, so get washed out in the troposphere but CFCs are insoluble in rain so they diffuse into the stratosphere. Here they are bombarded by UV light which breaks the chlorine atom from the molecule. These rogue chlorine atoms bond with the single oxygen atoms that otherwise would re-form ozone. This reduces the amount of ozone in the stratosphere and lets the harmful UV radiation reach ground level.

The enhanced greenhouse effect (troposphere)

Note that the problem with the ozone layer is to do with letting UV through the stratosphere, with the resultant damage to living cells below. In contrast, the greenhouse effect is to do with the absorption in the troposphere of infra-red radiation ('radiant heat') *from* the Earth's surface, preventing it from escaping to outer space.

The glass in a greenhouse lets visible sun-light through. Some of this light is absorbed by the soil which gets hot and 'glows' with infra-red radiation, often called radiant heat. The infra-red radiation (heat) given off from the soil cannot get through glass, so heat energy is built up in the greenhouse. It is the same effect as in a car left in the sun with its windows shut.

Gases such as carbon dioxide and water vapour make our atmosphere act like a greenhouse. They let the light from the sun through, and the ground gets hot, but they absorb the infra-red (IR) radiation from the warmed Earth, preventing it all from escaping to outer space. This is a good thing – without this natural 'greenhouse' effect the Earth would not be warm enough to support life. But humankind is upsetting the balance by putting more carbon dioxide (and other 'greenhouse' gases) into the troposphere, increasing the natural greenhouse effect and causing global warming. For more discussion of the energy balance see Chapter 6.

We need to remember that **fuel** and **oxygen** are needed for burning. Since normal (hydro-carbon) fuels contain the elements carbon and hydrogen, the products which are built up during burning are the oxides of carbon (carbon dioxide, CO_2) and of hydrogen (water, H_2O). Every tonne of coal burnt adds more than three tonnes of carbon dioxide to the atmosphere. If you prevent the growth of plants, by cutting down trees, you destroy one way this build-up of carbon dioxide could be reduced.

An increase in global temperatures, 'Global Warming', may be harmful to ecosystems, which take time to adapt to changing climatic conditions. The extra energy retained by the atmosphere will lead to greater extremes of weather – more violent storms etc. In addition, glacier and Antarctic ice cap melting and expansion of the seas as they warm up will lead to coastal flooding.

In our teaching we need to emphasise combustion as a constructive process in which air joins with the fuel and produces gases. Although these gases are usually invisible the water vapour often condenses, as in car exhausts, and this provides clear evidence of new materials being produced (in this case, harmless). If you put a jar over a burning candle the candle eventually goes out. The gases in the jar are no longer the same as fresh air, shown by placing this jar over another lighted candle which goes out immediately. Burning rubbish and fuels pumps invisible exhaust gases into the atmosphere, and we need children to understand that these contribute to the enhanced greenhouse effect.

Acid rain (troposphere)

Although living things are made mostly of the elements carbon, hydrogen and oxygen, they also contain small amounts of nitrogen, sulphur, phosphorus and several other 'trace' elements. Fossil fuels are derived from living things, and still contain these additional elements, especially sulphur. You may have heard of 'low sulphur fuels' (e.g. North Sea oil) which can be sold at a premium. They contain less than 1 per cent sulphur. Petrol has a very low sulphur content. It is the burning of coal and heavy fuel oils that contribute mostly to sulphur dioxide in the atmosphere.

When fuels burn they combine with oxygen, and all the elements in the fuel are built up into oxides. Carbon dioxide and water (oxides of carbon and hydrogen) comprise the bulk of these, but sulphur dioxide can make up to 4 or 5 per cent of the chimney stack fumes.

Nitrogen oxides have a different source. If you burn living matter on a bonfire its nitrogen content is released as the gas, elemental nitrogen. The temperature is not high enough for nitrogen oxide to form. Thus an agriculture based on slash and burn, although retaining many trace metallic elements in the ash, loses the vital nitrogen. Wood ash is a good fertiliser, but lacks nitrogen – only composting, or biogas production, retains the nitrogen.

Plants cannot absorb nitrogen directly from the air though some bacteria, such as those in the root nodules of legumes such as beans and peas, can. During lightning flashes small amounts of nitrogen and oxygen in the atmosphere join to form nitrogen oxide providing another important way of 'fixing' nitrogen for plants. Under the extremes of temperature involved in the burning of petrol in motor vehicles, the same reaction occurs and some of the nitrogen (which makes up 80 per cent of the air used for combustion) combines with oxygen, and the exhaust gases contain small, but significant, amounts of nitrogen oxides.

Burning organic material can produce solid ash and gaseous exhausts. Ash is made from metallic oxides, is alkaline and is used to 'sweeten' the soil, whereas non-metal oxides are gases, appear in exhausts and give rise to acids when they dissolve in rain water. The release of these non-metal oxides into the atmosphere, especially oxides of nitrogen and sulphur, results in acid deposition. If the soils are naturally alkaline the sulphur and nitrogen simply add to the fertility of the soil, otherwise acidity can build up and cause damage to ecosystems.

To understand why changes in acidity are so harmful, we need to remember that few changes can take place in living cells without enzymes, These are the biological catalysts and they have a delicate 3-D structure built of protein. Each reaction has its own unique enzyme, with its own unique shape, allowing it to facilitate very specific chemical changes in the molecules of life. The shape of enzymes is held by weak bonds which can be disturbed in a process called denaturing. This commonly happens if the cell gets too hot (the enzyme is shaken too violently) but changes in acidity are also the cause of shape change, causing the enzyme to stop working.

We all know that acid conditions are used to prevent microbes from working – we call the preservation method *pickling*. Acid rain has the same effect on life in general, first picking off the most sensitive creatures, then gradually nearly all life ceases, as the acidity levels increase.

In addition to damage to enzymes, the highly acid conditions cause toxic metal salts, normally not soluble, to dissolve and damage living things. Metallic elements play an important, indeed *essential*, part in living things. We take iron for blood, calcium for bones. Potassium is included in plant fertiliser, and zinc supplements are prescribed by doctors. Metals such as iron and zinc form the active site in many enzymes (for example iron in the oxygen carrying protein called haemoglobin, *haima* = Greek for blood). Toxic metals, such as aluminium, cadmium, lead and mercury, are chemically similar to *essential* metals, so 'mimic' them, but then they are unable to play the full part of the metal they mimic. If they are brought into solution by acid conditions the living thing is damaged.

Atmosphere summary – what can we do?

Substances we discard that are caught up into the atmospheric cycles can occasionally be incorporated into natural processes, such as water vapour from use of fuel, and acid rain on alkaline soils. Mostly, however, no mechanism exists to remove the volatile pollutants we throw away, and ecosystems are damaged: by UV (from ozone depletion); by global warming (from carbon dioxide emissions); or by acid deposition. Action has now been taken to stop manufacture of CFCs and other ozone depleters through the Montreal protocol. Global agreement to reduce carbon dioxide emissions appears a long way off, though the Rio summit made a start. Cleaning up acidity in exhausts, on cars and powerstation stacks is well under way. All cost money, all require restraint, but if the next generation understand the science behind them they will understand the need for action.

Rocks (geology)

Our time on this planet is so short in geological terms that it is hardly feasible to consider the rock cycle as a means to recycle our rubbish. Ocean floors, made from basaltic rocks, are continually being made at mid-ocean ridges. No ocean floor is much older than 100 million years, which means that they have been renewed about 50 times since the formation of the planet. In contrast the continents, made mainly from less dense granitic rock, are as old as the planet itself, conveyed around the surface of the Earth on tectonic plates like lumps of ice floating on water. Where two plates meet deep ocean trenches form as ocean crust is subducted, and any continental crust gets piled up in great folds of mountains, like the Himalayas or Alps. Along these plate boundaries we get volcanic activity and earthquakes. The formation of sediment, weathered from the continents and eroded down to the seas recycles a little of the continent – some of this is folded up as plates meet, and some gets dragged down, only to melt and get squeezed up in volcanic activity.

In millions of years time sediments of our own life-style will remain as fossil evidence in the rocks, just as we learn of dinosaurs and early humans from the record they left in the rocks. Maybe later life forms will mine these seams for useful materials, just as we dig up the fossil forests of the carboniferous period, 300 million years after they were formed.

Life (biology)

During the 18th century scientists realised that living things were made of the same matter as that from which their environment is composed. Children need experience that plants obtain all they need from air, water and soil, and that this material is passed on to animals. Living things return materials to the environment to be used over and over again. Materials from life (wood, cotton etc) are biodegradable so can be recycled through the action of microbes after use. Synthetic life-polymer materials however, are not and must be recycled in other ways.

Figure 5.3 is a simplification of the way materials are cycled by living things. All material of life begins as small molecules that are built up into life-polymers to form the structure of the living thing. This building process requires energy, so more small molecules are needed as fuel, usually also needing oxygen. Plants get their small molecules from the water, air and soil that surrounds them, a process that starts with photosynthesis. Animals rely on other living things for their small molecules, so their first task is to break down the life polymer structure in their food in a process we call digestion. The decomposing fungi and bacteria do just that to the biodegradable material we throw away, as they do to the leaves that fall in autumn.

It is important for children to see digestion and decomposition in this light – they are energy requiring processes that produce small molecules from the giant structures of life. Living things then do two things with these small molecules. They either use them for growth, building them back into polymers again, an energy requiring process, or they use them as a fuel, in an energy releasing process called respiration.

In a nut-shell that is what life does. As long as the materials we throw away are biodegradable, meaning that microbes can break them up into useable bits, they will be brought back into the natural cycles of life. Thus jute fishing nets, leather boots, paper bags and wooden buttons are food for microbes. We should discourage the term 'broken down' (implying that they disappear?) and instead remember that they become broken up or apart, enabling them to be used for growth and as a fuel for the decomposing organisms.

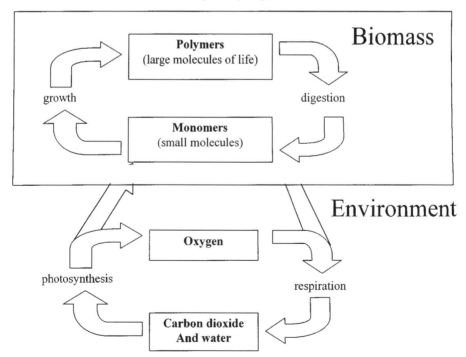

Figure 5.3 The cycling of materials by living things

Life-polymers that are manufactured from petrochemicals, such as nylon, polythene and Formica, have molecular structures that are not the right shape for the digestion enzymes of decomposers, so they lie un-rotted as unsightly rubbish, and are lost to the material cycles. For these materials we need to develop our own cycles, either re-using them (shopping bags) re-cycling them (plastic bottle bank) or developing our own chemical digester (e.g. through pyrolysis – decomposition at high temperatures) to break them up into small molecules for re-use. We cannot wait a million years whilst evolution produces microbes that will recognise nylon and use it as their food.

In the next section we will consider the energy sources that drive these great cycles of matter.

Fuelling cycles

The collection and re-cycling of rubbish requires effort, and must be fuelled. That is why it is easier to drop our rubbish on the pavement or dump it in holes in the ground. The three natural cycles described above all need energy to function, and we also require an energy source to cycle our own materials when there is no natural cycle to do the work for us. This section considers these energy sources.

The main source is the sun, which drives life and climate, and causes the rocks to be weathered and transported to form new sediment. Energy from the primordial heat and radioactivity that keeps the rocks molten deep within the Earth provides the energy to move the Earth's tectonic plates. The gravitational forces between the Earth and the moon cause the oceans to rise and fall. This tidal motion, from the gravitational potential energy and kinetic energy of the Earth–Moon system, causes some coastal erosion and can provide a small renewable addition to our stock of useful energy.

The sun

The sun drives living things through photosynthesis, and drives climate and weather systems by heating the Earth and evaporating water. It also plays a part in the rock cycle during weathering and erosion.

The sun drives living things

The daily input of high grade electromagnetic radiation from sunlight drives living systems through photosynthesis. Carbon dioxide and water, taken in by green plants, are pulled apart by energy from the sun captured by the chlorophyll molecule (a protein structure, similar to haemoglobin, but using magnesium as the active site metal) to form oxygen and small organic molecules (such as sugar). These small molecules either get built up into life structures needed to form the plant, often using additional elements such as nitrogen and phosphorus from the minerals obtained from the soil (growth), or they get used as a fuel (respiration). Energy becomes available to life through respiration when the biomass, or fuel, rejoins with oxygen to form carbon dioxide and water once again. Animals rely on ready-grown biomass for their source of growth materials and fuel, by feeding on other life-forms. Warm-blooded active animals, such as mammals, may use 90 per cent of their food intake for fuel, and only 10 per cent as material for growth and repair. Less active animals use their food more efficiently, so more is passed on as new biomass, and less is respired to reform carbon dioxide and water.

Human technology makes use of solar replenishable energy through use of human muscles (walking, the bicycle), animal muscle power (horse and cart), the burning of wood, etc.

The sun drives climatic systems and part of the rock cycle

The sun's energy absorbed by the surface of the oceans causes water to evaporate. Convection currents are driven by energy from the sun heating up the land or sea causing air to get warm – it pushes back the surrounding cold air as it expands. Colder denser air now pushes it up away from the surface, causing the hot air, despite its weight, to rise against gravity. Winds thus formed carry the water to the mountains where it is dropped. Winds blow, causing waves and sand storms. Convection currents in the oceans are driven by sunlight in a similar way. The rotation of the Earth helps to stir things up too. The recycled water, in the form of rain, is vital to life on the land and is kept going by the sun. We trap some of this available replenishable energy through waterwheels, hydroelectric schemes, windmills and turbines, yachts and wave power.

Rocks are broken into bits, or weathered, by the action of ice, wind, rain, and the growth of plants, all supplied with energy from the sun. The broken bits are transported, or eroded, by wind and water, eventually ending up in the sea or other sediments. Over time they consolidate and form hard sedimentary rock.

Geothermal/nuclear

Heat energy from the Earth's interior drives convection cycles in the magma which cause the major plate activity forming the other half of the rock cycle. The energy from the Earth's centre is maintained by nuclear processes, without which the centre would by now be much cooler than it is. This heat energy is available as a renewable resource to technology as hot springs and geothermal power.

Fossil fuel/oxygen systems

Biomass formed by photosynthesis millions of years ago, which then failed to recombine with oxygen, was trapped underground as fossil fuels. These form a non-renewable energy resource, made available to technology through burning (where the fossilised biomass rejoins with oxygen to form carbon dioxide and water once again).

The use of fossil fuels releases humankind from relying on the daily ration of solar energy, but the huge increase in their use has had a serious impact on ecosystems, both from resource exploitation (oil spills, mining spoils, etc), and the climatic consequences of releasing carbon dioxide and acidic oxides into the atmosphere. A majority of people on this planet live by using almost only those fuels produced by renewable energy from the sun: like all other living things such people are 'prisoners of the sun'. But as long as they plant trees to replace those used as firewood, and as long as grasslands survive the cropping of draught animals, theirs is a sustainable and renewable way of life.

If all of humanity were to live only from energy from respiration of our food, all our complex technological systems would collapse into chaos. The next chapter considers the energy crisis in more detail.

Fuelling material cycles – summary

The maintenance of a highly ordered system, like life or our technological world, requires the constant input of high grade energy. If we want to avoid polluting our homes we must tidy up (at the expense of using fuels). If we want to avoid polluting the planet, we must recycle – also at the expense of using fuels. But fuels are made of matter, they join with oxygen forming oxides when they are 'used', so we must also include their use when we examine the matter cycles of the planet.

Consider now the difference between using replenishable sources of energy and using fossil fuels. As the sun shines on Earth its energy could just warm up the ground. Alternatively, the energy could be trapped by plants and provide us with many materials, such as paper, cotton, and food waste, which eventually end up as rubbish. If these are burnt or converted to methane in a digester and then burnt, useful energy can be obtained in the form of electricity for our vacuum cleaner. This energy degrades to waste heat as it is 'used'. The amount of carbon dioxide released during combustion is the same as that which was trapped by the plants not so long before. The net result is identical to the sun shining on the ground – the amount of carbon dioxide remains unchanged, and the Earth gets a little warmer, as it does in the day. This heat is lost at night, and the Earth remains in balance (see Figure 5.4):

Everything we do has an energy cost. What is the cost of aluminium except that it has required the burning of fuel: to dig ore from the ground, to transport it to the smelting works, to extract it, to purify it, to transport it to the can-making factory, to manufacture drinks cans, to transport them to be filled . . .?

What we must do is to minimise the energy cost of maintaining our material cycles. In the end we must accept that on this planet we have a constant, but limited input of solar energy, which, together with other replenishable resources we need to develop, must be used to keep all materials we use in a cycle. Life on Earth has managed to survive for over 3000 million years using this principle, and we escape it now at our peril.

We have provided a picture of life on the planet fuelled by solar energy, helped by enzymes, where all materials are re-used, and nothing is wasted. This picture is moderated by the slow accumulation of biomass trapped where there is no oxygen, forming peat. From other ages this trapped biomass is now

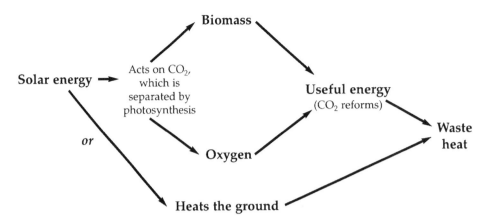

Figure 5.4 Natural degradation of solar energy

available to us as fossil fuel. Although it may have taken millions of years to be formed, we are using it up over mere hundreds of years. It is our escape from the limitations of solar energy that has led to the enormous resource and pollution problems associated with our use of materials. We will need even more fuel to provide proper cycles for these materials.

The chapter ends with a case study of the way we use materials in the home. Many of these investigations can be used with children to help them appreciate some of the bigger, global issues discussed above. By considering our home as a microcosm of the Earth we can bring some reality of the underlying issues to the children we teach.

Case study 3: A materials audit for the home

It is easy to think of materials entering and leaving the home as if it was a one way trip – shopping, water and fuel come in and other things leave via the refuse bin and the drains. In addition, we don't always think of materials surviving in full once they are used. Thus food may be reduced to faeces, gas and coal burnt to nothing, cleansing agents such as soap getting 'used up'. This case study tries to do a complete audit on the materials that enter and leave our home. If the Lego brick model of matter is appropriate, we must account for all the bricks that come in and match them with the bricks that leave.

Volatiles: water

Water may be the easiest material to account for. In it comes clean, out it goes, down the drain, dirty. It is a fairly common idea that the water in a river is drunk several times before it reaches the sea, though the idea that the sewage works out-flow is the water intake for the next town downstream is hard to stomach sometimes. The distillation of the sea water by the sun, allowing it to rain and renew the river, completes this story.

Not all the water comes in through the mains – there's rain water, and there's the water we buy for drinking, such as beer and pop. And not all leaves by the drain – we lose body water when sweat evaporates, and evaporation comes from bathing, cleaning and cooking too. The amount is small, and leaves the house through the doors and windows as invisible water vapour.

Solids: food, packaging and cleaning materials

Neglecting capital items used to repair or build your home, the main classes of solids that we bring in are as follows:

- Life polymers (biodegradable) – food, newspaper, paper/card packaging. We could include solid fuels here, but they can be dealt with when we consider gas.
- Life polymers (non-biodegradable) – plastic packaging such as bags, boxes, pots and bottles.
- Rocks – glass bottles and jars.
- Metals – aluminium foil and cans, iron 'tins', battery cases.
- Volatiles – cleansing and skin care materials such as soap, detergent, deodorant, makeup, bleach.
- Ionic – very little, except cooking and water softening salt, and soda. Also the electrolyte ('acid') in electrical cells (torch batteries).

Packaging materials and newspapers

Packaging materials and newspapers leave the house in the bin, somewhat crumpled but in a form much the same as they came in. Our main task here is to encourage children and their parents to re-use, or recycle as much as possible. European legislation now requires large companies to account for their packaging, and they pay heavily if there is not a recycling system for it. We are beginning to see recycling bins at all supermarkets and some car parks, but few local authorities have achieved the well organised waste collection systems seen in some European countries, with different bags for metal, plastic, organic biodegradable waste, newspapers and glass. Once the rubbish has been mixed it takes additional energy resources to unmix it, and clean it, ready for recycling.

Some companies allow you to refill containers rather than throwing them away after a single use. Famous for this is our doorstep milk delivery, where the same glass bottles make the trip over and over again. We used to do the same with shopping bags, and some supermarkets encourage customers to re-use stronger bags, for which they make a charge. If it were illegal to give plastic bags away free in shops and we were made to pay 10p per bag we would quickly be encouraged to use a strong permanent shopping bag.

Food and drink

Much of our food is water, which we incorporate into our own cells as we grow, or filter it out of our blood and pass it down the drain in our urine. The nutritious part of the food, mainly carbohydrate, fat and protein, gets broken up into bits small enough to enter the blood by the process called digestion.

About 90 per cent of the food we absorb into the blood is used as a fuel – the sugars (from digestion of starch) and the fats. We also breath in oxygen (see gases below) which enters the blood in our lungs. These two, the fuel and oxygen, are available to all the cells in our body, which are constantly respiring in order to provide themselves with energy. Starve the brain of oxygen for more than five minutes and the brain dies. The fuel and oxygen join, forming carbon dioxide and water and these travel back to the lungs (and kidneys) to be excreted. Few adults or children will be able to answer the question 'Where does most of the food we digest leave the body?' with an answer 'from our lungs and out of our mouth and nose', yet this is a simple and important picture, showing that matter, despite chemical and biological changes, is never destroyed at an atomic level. It does not turn into energy, but is still there, the carbon in the carbohydrate picking up oxygen to form carbon dioxide and the hydrogen forming water.

The other 10 per cent of our digested food provides the material for building our bodies. New cells need plenty of protein, built up from amino acids, and they need nucleic acids to make new DNA. When we digest our food these building blocks are formed and enter the blood. Although children will retain some of these materials as they grow bigger, old cells are continually dying. As adults we eat but (usually) get no heavier. So where does the material go which is replaced by the new intake of structural material? The answer is on the floor or down the drain. Dead cells from our skin flake off and stick to our clothes or fall to the floor. When the clothes or our bodies are washed the dead cells get washed down the drain. The cells on the floor form part of house dust, and provide food for dust mites. From there some will be respired back into the air, the rest will be built into new mites.

The bits of our food that we cannot or do not digest, together with dead cells from our gut, pass out virtually unchanged as faeces. These settle out in the sewage works and, through anaerobic bacteria in digester tanks, provide methane as a fuel for generating electricity, so the carbon ends up back in the air. The remains can be spread on fields to provide humus for the soil.

Volatiles: cleansing materials

Aerosols are now powered by propane, where once CFCs were used. The propane is highly inflammable, but quickly spreads out in the air, where it slowly oxidises to carbon dioxide and water. The other material in the can, the one you want, such as deodorant, will also evaporate and spread out in the air, to be washed out later by the rain, and some will stick to your body, eventually going down the drain. Cleansers, disinfectants and bleaching agents may leave your house cleaner, but they all end up at the sewage works. Washing powders contain phosphates, which act as a nutrient for plant (algal) growth in rivers, and the soaps and surfactants, used to get water to penetrate your clothes, cause foam formation in sewage outfalls. The more you try to make your house clean, the more materials you add to the sewage, and the bigger the problem becomes for the next town's water supply inlet, and for life in the river. Bacteria only become a problem in a house if they are given a good food supply and warm conditions. If food falls on the floor or onto a kitchen surface it may pick up a few bacteria. It is only if it is then left in the warm to fester that it becomes hazardous to eat. We use far too much and too many cleansing materials, in the kitchen, in the bathroom, on our bodies. They all end up placing additional stress on the environment.

Volatiles: gases – fuel and air

Air comes into and out of the house through doors and windows. Although much remains the same we must remember the role of oxygen in respiration and burning. For every kg of fuel you burn (about a cubic metre of gas) you will produce nearly 3 kg of carbon dioxide. This will go up the chimney or flue (for a central heating boiler or fire) or enter the air from a gas cooker. For every kg of carbohydrate that enters your blood you will need to breathe out about one and a half kg of carbon dioxide. Carbon dioxide from the fossil fuel will add to the greenhouse effect. Your own carbon dioxide will be recycled as the next season's crops grow.

Summary

There is much that can be done in the primary school to lay the foundations of this picture of the materials we use. If the issues are not addressed, early misconceptions are built firmly into the child's understanding, simply from observing everyday events around them, where they see materials coming and going, some disappearing and others appearing apparently at will.

At Key Stage 1 we can give experience of the range of solids, showing that each has a source, a life history. At Key Stage 2 gases can be introduced as real heavy materials, which just happen to be more spread out than the condensed states of solid and liquid. Many changes, such as evaporation and burning, can be shown to conserve matter only when the concept of material gases had been taken on board. Although chemical changes, such as burning, digestion and respiration are introduced formally only at KS3, the Lego model of matter can begin to give primary school children this sense of continuity. The water cycle is easily appreciated at KS2, but the need for cycles for all matter can also be introduced, and the re-cycling schemes, increasingly being run by schools, can help to develop this global understanding.

The above case study of the materials entering and leaving a house can also be tackled at primary school. Not all the parts will be understood, but the big idea of indestructibility of matter (at a lego brick level) will begin to take shape, and the impact of loading the environment with all our discarded materials will begin to sink in.

Chapter 6

Energy and fuels

Keith Ross

Introduction

The revised National Curriculum fought shy of mentioning energy at Key Stages 1 and 2 (DfE 1995). The authors thought the concept was too complex to be tackled with young children. We argue in this chapter that not only is energy a very approachable concept, once we take the confusions and misconceptions into account, but also it is a word used by most five year olds, and if we don't develop their understanding during their primary years the misconceptions and confusions will remain with them.

Popular use (and misuse) of the word *energy* has led to two major confusions in the language associated with it. These confusions are easily illustrated by thinking about what is happening in Figure 6.1.

Figure 6.1 Hungry person question

The middle picture shows someone being energetic – even young children will be happy to say there is energy here (movement energy). The questions are:

1. Where did this energy go to (third picture)? Is any energy left?
2. And where did it come from (first picture)? Is there any energy in the first picture?

The first two sections in this chapter deal with these two fundamental questions about energy. We then look more widely at the energy words we use, and try to give them some meaning. Finally we attempt to construct an energy audit for our homes and for the Earth itself.

Is energy used up (tackling question one)?

If you answer this question by saying that the person has used up their energy, which needs to be replenished, you are using the word energy in its everyday sense.

Nowadays, the word 'energy' has come to represent an ability to do something *useful* and is best represented in science by saying something has 'fuel value'. It is in this everyday sense that energy (or, at least, its fuel-value or usefulness) can be used up. According to scientists, however, energy is measured in joules and does not change in amount, but simply becomes transferred from one form to another. There is movement energy, electrical energy, heat energy, radiation (e.g. light), sound etc.

An environmentally aware politician might say, 'Energy (fuel-value) is being used up, so we must conserve it, and use it wisely.' A scientist, on the other hand, might say, 'When something happens the total amount of energy (joules) does not change, so the amount of energy in the universe is constant – it is conserved.'

This double meaning (fuel-value needs conserving or joules are conserved) can cause major problems for learners when their teachers are unaware that the words *energy* and *conservation* mean different things in both cases. We need to consider the laws of *thermodynamics* to understand this. These laws are not obscure highly technical scientific ideas, but a simple statement of what is common sense.

When the scientist says energy is transferred from one form to another she is applying the **first law of thermodynamics** and is what we often learn in school: the amount of energy, measured in joules, remains the same – energy cannot be created or destroyed. Thus chemical energy from respiring your food is transferred into movement and heat. Energy may be wasted but none is lost or used up.

Let us consider a 100 watt light bulb as a simpler example. This is supplied with 100 joules of electrical energy in one second. The electrical energy supplied to the light bulb is transferred into light and heat. The first law says that if you add up the amount of energy supplied as electricity it will be equal to the amount given out as light and lost as heat.

Flow diagrams, so-called 'Sankey' diagrams, can be useful to help account for the energy during any change (see Figure 6.2). Here the height of the box represents the 100 joules of electrical energy, and a box of the same height after the filament bulb shows that we still have 100 joules, but in the form of heat (97 joules) and light (3 joules). Figure 6.2 also shows that with the 'low energy' bulb only 10 joules come in as electrical energy and we still get 3 joules of light, but only 7 joules are wasted as heat.

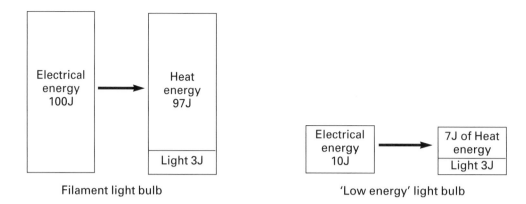

Figure 6.2 Sankey diagrams

For practical purposes, then, the 97 per cent of the energy of the filament bulb is wasted, in common language the energy is used up, and only 3 per cent comes out as useful light energy. Even this 3 per cent does not last. Once you switch off the electrical supply the light also stops – where has it gone? Light from the bulb hits the walls and objects in the room and is partially absorbed (making the walls slightly warmer). Any light reflected is rapidly absorbed in subsequent rebounds so unless we continually supply the room with new light energy it rapidly gets dark. (It is interesting to compare this to much slower travelling sound; in a cave sound will take several seconds to be fully absorbed.) The energy that is now in the form of heat is useless to us, so we ignore it. In everyday terms the electrical energy has been used up, and we have to buy more electricity from the supplier.

This everyday life description of energy becoming useless is an expression of the **second law of thermodynamics**. The electricity ends up as waste heat in the walls and items in the room. In our more complex example, once the food has been respired in the cells of our body, or petrol is burnt in a car, the energy transferred becomes scattered as waste heat, through friction during movement, and movements of air, and it cannot be used any more. Even reception infants know this. This transcript is from Ross and Lakin (1998) and the children are talking about what makes a car go:

> Teacher: *What happens to the petrol in the car?*
> Child(ren): it goes out of the back.
> Teacher: *What do you mean it goes out of the back?*
> Child(ren): 'zorst pipe/it makes/goes into smoke and goes out the zorst pipe to make the engine go/to make the car go.
> Teacher: *Can you collect the petrol again from the exhaust pipe?*
> Child(ren): no no/no/only from the station.

We see this progression from a concentrated useful resource to scattered waste all around us, with matter as well as with energy. Rooms become untidy, bath water becomes dirty, electricity lights our homes and the energy becomes scattered waste heat. It is the second law at work: the universe becomes less ordered and everything spreads out and muddles up over time. For a room to remain tidy there has to be a daily input of energy, e.g. from muscle power or a vacuum cleaner, but as the matter in the room becomes ordered and useful again, the energy you 'use' is degraded and becomes useless. Scientists have coined the word *entropy* for this – a measure of disorder. Entropy increases with time, and we need a constant input of high grade energy to keep the place tidy.

The interesting systems on Earth – life and climate for example – are highly ordered and complex, we might say they have a low entropy. In order to retain their complex structure they must be constantly fuelled, just as it takes constant effort to keep a house tidy. It is the sun that provides this constant input of high grade energy. You only need to consider the ferocity of a storm or a forest fire to see the enormous amount of 'fuel-value' energy locked up in our climatic or living systems. We need to look at the science of complexity (see Chapter 7) to understand how life on Earth has evolved into its complex nature over time, but the maintenance of this order is only possible with this solar input of high-grade fuel-value energy.

Combining the two meanings we can say: as this 'energy' is 'used' it degrades into waste heat, so we have to come back for more. In this way energy can be seen as a flow, from high grade, useful sources to scattered waste heat. This is unlike the matter cycles we met in Chapter 5, where matter (at an atomic level) cannot be destroyed. We have to develop, and supply fuel for, cycles for all those materials we use that cannot be recycled by natural means.

Renewable energy refers to high grade energy sources which are constantly replenished – on Earth the major source is the sun, which fuels both life and the climatic systems. Renewable is the wrong word to use, because the energy is not re-used. Because it transfers to waste heat, we have to come back for more, just as the children said above about the cars going to the petrol station. The sun shines with new energy everyday: it is replenished. The heated Earth 'glows' from this warming, and heat is radiated away into outer space. The energy lost as heat is equal to the energy gained as sunlight so the temperature of the Earth remains roughly constant. If the heat cannot escape so easily, for example when we pump greenhouse gases into the atmosphere, the earth has to get a few degrees warmer to get rid of the waste heat and we call this global warming.

Until very recently humans were 'prisoners of the sun' (BBC 2, 1992) relying solely on water power, animal and human muscle power, burning wood, and the power of the wind: to move them about (horses and sailing ships), to prepare their food (wind-mills, wood fires), and work their fields (bullock plough). All these energy resources are replenished by the sun.

During the industrial revolution we gradually freed ourselves from relying on present day sunlight, and began to use up fossil fuel deposits. They were formed over millions of years, but are being used up over hundreds of years, so they are non-renewable. This is the energy crisis. It is not about a lack of energy itself (measured in joules), but about the coming shortage of sources of high quality energy.

To summarise so far: there are two distinct meanings of the word *energy*. One (measured in joules) is only known to scientists, and is a quantity that remains unaffected during changes. The other is the meaning it has in everyday language.

It is what 'makes things go' and is close to the scientists' idea of a driving force. Energy is only useful when it is highly ordered and concentrated, and becomes 'used up' by becoming scattered.

With this understanding you should appreciate why we are being urged to 'save it' – not the scientists' energy measured in joules, but its *usefulness.*

Is there energy in food and fuels? (tackling question two)

Surely, you will say, there is energy in fuels – all the text books say so, and anyway it is common knowledge that when fuels burn 'their energy' is released: 'Food gives you energy', '. . . fuel contains energy', '. . . energy in petrol', '. . . energy of the fuel', '. . . energy is stored in food molecules', or worse, '. . . energy is stored in the bonds'. All these imply that there is energy in the fuel or food. This idea perpetuates the myth that when food is eaten or fuels burn they 'turn into energy'. Yet fuels and food are made only of atoms. As these remain after the fuels have been used, how can they 'contain' energy, and in what way are they 'used up'?

This section looks at the origin of energy associated with fuels more carefully, and examines the way the presently accepted view that 'fuels contain energy' acts as a barrier to understanding – a barrier that begins to be built even with the reception infants above who know that the car needs petrol to make it go.

Where is the energy if it is not in the food and fuels?

So where is the energy that is supposed to be in fuels? Many people say it is *released when the bonds break* – but bonds hold atoms together and it requires an *input* of energy to break them apart. To find a better answer we must remember that both fuel *and oxygen* are needed if energy is to be released. We argue that fuels do not contain energy but rather 'the energy *is associated with the fuel–oxygen system.*'

Unless we bring our pupils to a clearer picture of where this energy does come from, and how it is stored, we cannot hope that they will understand the interplay of matter and energy in living things. Instead we shall continue to have people thinking that when fuels burn, or food is respired, they turn into energy, or somehow crack open, releasing their 'store of energy'. People who are unaware of the combustion products we breathe out or which go up the chimney.

Survey results (Ross 1989) show that people go through several stages in coping with the conservation of matter: a young child may think the amount of solid matter can change (on shape change or crushing to a powder), while an older child may think matter disappears when it dissolves. However most children and many adults find it hard to imagine gases as being made of real stuff and think of air as weightless (see Chapter 5). Indeed, historically chemists took a long time to think of gases as material substances, rather than 'unweighable aethers'. Until gases are seen as being made of the same stuff as solids and liquids, chemistry is nonsense. It is harder still to believe that matter is conserved during *chemical* change. This is addressed in the following question:

Suppose we could trap all the fumes etc. from the exhaust pipe of a car and were able to weigh them – e.g. by compressing them into a gas bottle. We would then be able to compare the amount of petrol used during a journey with the amount of exhaust collected at the end.

Would the mass of exhaust be:
(a) much larger than . . .
(b) about the same as . . . .
or (c) much smaller than . . . the mass of petrol used?

Many people answer this question by saying the mass of the exhaust gases would be *smaller*. The reason they give is 'matter is converted into energy' – the fuel is an energy source, so it must be 'used up'. They may also believe that gases are weightless, but the question is phrased in a way that tries to avoid this response. Those who say the exhaust must have the same mass as the petrol at least realise that what goes in must come out. But that is not the whole story of the exhaust gas in the question – it is a select few who realise that the mass must be much larger because of the oxygen that has been added.

If matter is not turned to energy what is the origin of the energy released by burning fuels? Three possible answers could be (a) The fuel turns into energy (b) The energy is released when bonds in the fuel or food break and (c) Energy comes from making new bonds.

We have already dismissed response (a) because matter does not turn into energy. Many people answer this question by saying energy is released when bonds break – response (b). But we have already said that bonds *bond* – they glue atoms together, so it must cost energy to break bonds. It is when *weak bonds are replaced by stronger bonds* that there is a net release of energy. Oxygen atoms bond weakly with each other (in oxygen gas) but strongly with the atoms of carbon and hydrogen from the fuel (forming water and carbon dioxide), see Figure 6.3. So the energy is released from the *fuel–oxygen system*. That is why those who say there is energy *in fuel* or *in food* are perpetuating a serious misconception.

The petrol needs to react with oxygen. Most people know that cars need air filters, and that it is in the carburettor that fuel and air are mixed. The atoms in the fuel and air are not destroyed during chemical change, they just get rearranged. In this rearrangement the weak bonds in the oxygen (and fuel) molecules are replaced by stronger bonds in the water and carbon dioxide molecules. Figure 6.4 shows that when a car uses one kg of petrol it takes in about 15 kg of air (of which about 3.5 kg are oxygen), so 16 kg of exhaust are produced for every kg of petrol! A huge increase in mass over the petrol alone, but mass is still conserved if the fuel and air are both accounted for.

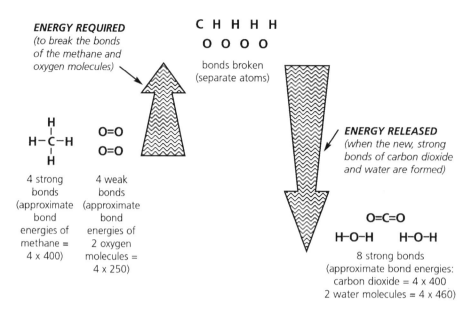

Figure 6.3 The origin of energy from fuels

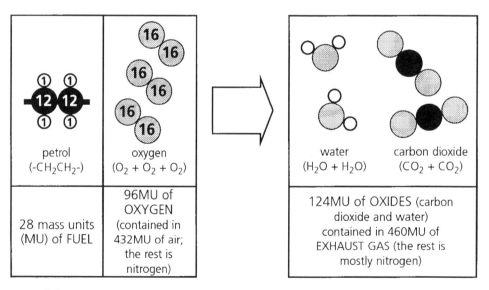

Figure 6.4 The mass of exhaust gases from a car.

If you scale this up you will see that each kilogram of petrol picks up about 3.5kg of oxygen (and a further 12kg of nitrogen, not shown). Including the nitrogen, the kilogram of petrol produces over 16kg of exhast gases. (Ross 1993)

Energy is stored in highly stretched oxides

Too little notice is taken of the part oxygen plays in the release of energy from food and fuels: the release of energy comes from allowing fuel and oxygen to join. Chemical energy arises from the breaking of weak bonds (in fuel and oxygen) and the making of strong ones (in exhaust fumes, carbon dioxide and water). There are the same number of atoms (and bonds) at the end as there were at the beginning of the change.

Think of it as keeping two reactive chemicals apart: allow them to spring together (fuel and oxygen for example) and energy is released. If you want to store energy in the system again, you have to pull the chemicals apart again (photosynthesis: pulling oxygen from oxides).

The origin of this energy is the sun. When sunlight falls on green leaves it fuels a process known as photosynthesis, in which the energy of sunlight acts on the oxides, carbon dioxide and water, and separates out the oxygen. This leaves biomass ('the stuff life is made of') behind in the leaf. In this way we could describe biomass, food, coal and other fossil fuels, together with the associated oxygen, as 'highly stretched carbon dioxide and water'. The link between the elastic forces of stretched springs and the electrostatic forces at an atomic level can be usefully made. During respiration and burning the biomass and oxygen rejoin, releasing the energy stored in this 'stretched spring'.

Instead of saying energy is some sort of substance that is found inside food and fuels we need to talk of **fuel–oxygen systems**. Matter, at a chemical (atomic) level, is distinct from energy and cannot be destroyed during chemical changes. The material in fuels cannot be turned into energy. (See Figure 6.3, above). Figure 6.5 is a highly simplified summary of the carbon cycle, showing, by keeping the thickness of the ring of circulating matter constant, that there is no loss of matter.

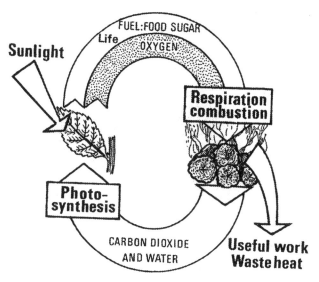

Figure 6.5 A simplified summary of the carbon cycle

Trophic levels

A few foxes feed on hundreds of rabbits, which rely on acres of grassland. Grass is the lowest trophic level (together with all green plants). The herbivores, like rabbits are the next level, and so on. It is well known that most of an animal's food is used as fuel. In the case of warm-blooded mammals, like rabbits, about 10 per cent is used for growth and so becomes available as new biomass at the next trophic level (food for the fox), and 90 per cent of the biomass is used as a fuel by recombining with oxygen and returning to the atmosphere.

Biology texts often talk of energy being passed along a food chain, or up trophic levels in an ecosystem. We should encourage them to talk of biomass being passed on, with a substantial part of it being used for respiration to fuel the organism, so returning the carbon to the atmosphere. It is not energy that is passed on, but fuel. Energy is transferred only through respiration of that food.

Implications for teaching

We read advertisements and cereal packets every day implying 'food contains energy'. This idea conflicts with a scientific understanding but is very persistent. In this section we suggest strategies that may help to overcome the misconceptions that children have about matter and energy that seem to last through their formal science education into adulthood. These are strategies to introduce ideas that are not only scientifically sound, but essential if we are to help the next generation towards a better understanding of their environment and how it works.

Our task, then, is to show children that the naive view has limited use, that is, the view that sees matter, and energy, as 'on-tap', with fuels turning into energy, and the unused bits becoming faeces or exhaust gases.

Emphasise the distinction between matter and energy

The main problem here is the way biomass (e.g. cornflakes, coal, fat, wood etc.) is called *energy*. Call it *fuel*, and emphasise that fuels usually need oxygen. Describe the energy associated with them as being very similar to the elastic energy stored in a spring – the spring has the same mass when stretched as when relaxed, just as the energy is stored when fuel and oxygen are kept apart and released as they join to re-form oxides.

Give evidence that gases are material substances

Flames, hot air, exhaust gases are often considered to be forms of energy. Certainly the life-world view is that they are weightless. We need to avoid such phrases as 'hot air rises' which suggests that it is not attracted by gravity, and say instead 'cold air sinks, because it is attracted more strongly by gravity to the earth.' There is a beautiful quotation from 1878 in Sutton (1992, p. 41) in which the air is described as 'an aerial ocean' round the earth in which 'birds swim and where people walk along the bottom.' We also need to get children to ask where matter goes during evaporation and burning.

Emphasise the constructive side to burning (combustion)

Our everyday experiences tell us that burning is a destructive process – only ashes remain. We must encourage pupils to see the exhaust gases which escape to the air as being massive, and to use this as evidence of an increase in mass as oxides are built up (see Figure 6.4). The same five year olds mentioned above (Ross 1991; Ross and Lakin 1998), when asked what happens to petrol in a car said: 'It goes into steam and it's all warm/'cos every time we cross the road I can feel it across my legs'. This is a rich and useful experience that needs to be built upon. Water is not often perceived to be a *product of combustion.* Nor, indeed, is the carbon dioxide we breathe out often perceived as an oxidation product of the food we eat, though the concern with the greenhouse effect is bringing the emission of carbon dioxide from burning of fossil fuels to the notice of the general public. Again, how many see the ashes left after a wood fire, as oxides of the metals that were taken in as minerals during the lifetime of the tree? Only when these oxide products of respiration and combustion are given more prominence will pupils begin to appreciate these as constructive processes.

Year 5/6 children may notice the condensation which collects inside a jar held above a burning candle. Many will say that this comes from the air when a cold surface (the glass) meets hot air (from the candle). But the jar is being heated – if you switch your rear windscreen heater on, or blow hot air from a hair dryer on your hair, do you find the rear window becomes misty, or the hair damp? You expect heating to drive water and dampness away, yet it collects above a hot burning candle.

Even the five year olds see the same condensation from the exhaust pipe of a car, and from our own breath. This water is a product of combustion. Fuels are hydrocarbons, or carbohydrates, containing the element hydrogen. When the fuel joins with oxygen during combustion or respiration hydrogen oxide (called water) forms as a product.

Emphasise the role played by air (oxygen)

If you want to get energy from food and fuels you need oxygen. Children know this from many everyday life experiences or stories. We take air with us under the sea or up a mountain because the brain can only survive for about five minutes without replenishing its supply of oxygen. A fire bursts into activity with the bellows, or can be coaxed back to life with judicious blowing. A candle, starved of air under a jar, goes out in a few seconds. Fire doors are kept closed to stop air getting to the fire. Chip-pan fires are extinguished by a fire blanket stopping the air reaching the fat.

Emphasise digestion as the process by which food enters the blood

Most text books show the alimentary canal going from mouth to anus – but the food's path is mouth – digestive system – blood – cells. If the food is used as fuel it then joins with oxygen, returns to the blood and leaves the body at the lungs (and as water in urine). Faeces are still fuel and used as food for other animals, and have never really entered the body. How many people answer the question 'Where does the food you eat leave the body?' with: 'From the lungs, in urine' and (for food used to replace body tissue) 'As house dust'. Most say (wrongly) 'It turns into energy and the rest comes out as faeces.'

A word of caution

Pupils' understanding in science is strongly influenced by what they do, see and hear in their everyday lives. If school science is to make any impact on their understanding, it must first of all recognise the influence of their everyday lives. It must not expect that one lesson will revolutionise their thoughts. Instead it must provide plenty of opportunity for pupils to translate the new ideas presented to them into their own words and meanings, and it must give the pupils opportunity to use and apply the new ideas, and give them the chance to compare the results with their existing ideas to show that these new ideas are better. The implications for teaching in the paragraphs above need to be learnt by every teacher, lest they fall back into the everyday speak of saying *food contains energy*.

Summary

The consequence of saying energy is in fuels is to imagine that energy is some sort of substance that is found inside food and fuels. It also makes people forget about the role of oxygen. They do not realise that the exhaust gases are, in consequence, much more massive than the fuel itself, and they build up in the atmosphere as possible pollutants. Matter, at an atomic level, is distinct from energy and cannot be destroyed during chemical changes, so fuels can neither contain, nor turn into energy.

The advantage of using the term *stretched oxides* is that it gives a much more realistic picture of how the energy is stored, and it forces you to see carbon dioxide and water as the beginning and end of the storing process – during photosynthesis the energy of sunlight pulls oxygen away from the carbon and hydrogen, forming biomass. Thus coal, fuels, food, biomass (and the associated oxygen), are highly stretched carbon dioxide and water. The link between the elastic forces of stretched springs and the electrostatic forces at an atomic level can be usefully made. During respiration and burning the biomass and oxygen rejoin, releasing the energy stored in this 'stretched spring'.

Instead of saying energy is some sort of substance that is found inside food and fuels we need to talk of *fuel–oxygen systems*. Matter, at a chemical (atomic) level, is distinct from energy and cannot be destroyed during chemical changes. The material in fuels cannot be turned into energy. Let's try to rephrase the quotations we began with:

'The process of *releasing energy from food and oxygen* is called respiration.'

'When coal is burned, chemical energy *associated with* the coal is converted into heat.'

'The energy previously used to *separate the fuel and oxygen* is released' [rather than *bond the molecules together*].

An energy audit for our home

When we examine the energy changes in a typical house we will need to apply all the ideas developed in this chapter. High grade energy will enter the house and an equal amount of low grade heat will leave, keeping the house at a constant temperature, and ensuring that all the matter in the house is kept clean and tidy. Matter is kept ordered whilst energy is degraded. Our aim is to 'use' as little of this high grade energy as possible, but still keep our house tidy and at a comfortable temperature. In this section we undertake this audit for a house in the UK in winter.

Energy inputs

Without the availability of fossil fuels, replenishable energy inputs will be from sunlight, from respiration of food and the burning of biomass. This allows us to see during the day, and do many jobs, by hand, around the house. With suitable clothing we can keep ourselves warm, but the house is likely to get very cold during the night. Wood fires and animal fat candles may allow some work to be done during the long hours of darkness.

In the modern house sunlight still provides an important input of heat and light during the day. Our bodies are kept at about 36 degrees centigrade, which is well above room temperature, and this is fuelled by respiration.

We supplement this replenishable energy by an input of electricity (most of which comes from burning fossil fuels) and by burning fossil fuels themselves (commonly natural gas). The energy we obtain from burning fossil fuel comes, as we discuss above, from allowing oxygen and fuel to join, forming carbon dioxide and water. Gas fires and central heating boilers produce so much exhaust gas that chimneys (flues) are used, which also carry away some of the heat since these exhaust gases are still hot. They also require large amounts of fresh air, which enter the house though air vents built into the walls or floor.

Energy outputs (losses)

At the end of a 24 hour period the house remains, on average, at the same temperature as it was previously. This means that all the energy that enters the house needs to leave it. All the energy we pay for in gas and electricity bills, and the replenishable energy from light and respiration, ends up in a slight heating of the air, water and ground around our house, but we have made some use of it as it scatters.

Let us examine this in a little more detail by considering the fate of the electrical energy transferred when using a one bar fire, a vacuum cleaner and the lights.

The fire (1000 watts)

The fire has a power of 1kilowatt, 1000 joules of energy every second. This warms the room, but since the room is warmer than the outside the room loses heat. A balance is struck, so that the room is kept at a constant temperature, and the energy from the fire spreads out, to the room and on. By insulating the house, escape of heat is slower and the room will get hotter before the balance is struck once more. Alternatively we could turn the fire off from time to time and maintain the original temperature.

The lights (typically 100 watts)

This 100 joules per second is transferred into light (3 joules) but mostly as heat (97 joules) (see Figure 6.2). The light is absorbed by things in the room which get marginally hotter. Our room now has an extra source of heat in it. By using 'low energy' light bulbs we can get the same 3 watts of brightness from only 10 watts. If everyone in the UK changed their most used bulb for a low energy bulb, we could shut a power station.

The vacuum cleaner (1000 watts)

The 1000 joules per second are transferred into movement of the working parts, movement of the air, to sound, and directly to heat. It is only the air movement, collecting up our dust, and the rotation of the brushes that is useful to us. The sound, the heat from the motor, and the heat from friction of the moving parts are all useless to us. Once the air has done its job it is pushed out into the room where its movement gradually becomes more random, and becomes heat. The vacuum cleaner, whilst it is being used, is heating the room as efficiently as the electric fire, but we are getting more use from the electricity before it degrades to heat.

Energy efficiency and global consequences of our house audit

Commonly, UK towns are a few degrees warmer than the countryside during winter because of this waste heat. We see snow lasting for less time in cities than in the surrounding countryside. Those houses which are not well insulated are the first to lose the layer of snow on their roof.

But perhaps the energy has not quite lost its usefulness. As the colder air from the country pushes the less dense warm town air away from the Earth, rising thermals of warm air are used by birds and glider pilots!

An energy audit for the Earth, with ideas for school

What we can explore with children in their own home can be extended to consider the whole planet as their experiences increase. We have four energy sources available to us to maintain our complex technological systems, as explained below:

The sun

The daily input of high grade electromagnetic radiation (emr) from the sun, i.e. light:

- drives living systems by separating biomass and oxygen during photo-synthesis; this becomes available to life through respiration (where the biomass rejoins with oxygen to form carbon dioxide and water once again), and to replenishable energy technology through use of animal muscle power, the burning of wood, etc;
- drives the climatic systems – wind, rain and ocean currents and the weathering of rocks; we trap some of this available energy through hydro-electric schemes, windmills and turbines, yachts and wave power.
- We also make direct use of sunlight, as a light and heat source during the day, in solar panels and in other solar technologies.

Fossil fuels

Biomass formed by photosynthesis millions of years ago, which then failed to recombine with oxygen, was trapped underground as fossil fuels. These form a non-replenishable energy resource, made available to technology through burning, where the fossilised biomass rejoins with oxygen to form carbon dioxide (now contributing to the enhanced greenhouse effect) and water once again.

Geothermal/nuclear

Heat energy from the Earth's interior drives convection cycles in the magma which cause the major plate activity of the rock cycle. This is available as a replenishable resource to technology as hot springs and geothermal power. We can also mine and concentrate radioactive uranium and obtain useful energy in nuclear power stations. Since the supply of these rocks is limited, nuclear power from uranium must be classed as a non-replenishable energy resource.

Gravitational

The gravitational forces between the Earth and the moon cause the oceans to rise and fall. This tidal motion can provide a small replenishable addition to our stock of useful energy.

Reducing our demand for high grade energy

The use of fossil fuels releases humankind from relying on the daily ration of solar energy, but the huge increase in its use has had a serious impact on ecosystems, both from resource exploitation (oil spills, mining spoils, etc), and the climatic consequences of releasing carbon dioxide and acidic oxides into the atmosphere. A majority of people on this planet live by using only those fuels produced by replenishable energy from the sun: like all other living things they are 'prisoners of the sun'. But as long as they plant trees to replace those used as firewood, and as long as grasslands survive cropping by draught animals, theirs is a sustainable and renewable way of life.

At the Rio conference in 1992 (see Chapter 7) nations agreed to reduce carbon dioxide emissions to the atmosphere in an attempt to reduce global warming. In order to meet our commitments (Department of the Environment 1995) the UK decided not to reduce energy demand, but instead swapped coal for gas. Natural gas is a hydrocarbon with a high hydrogen content, so when it burns it forms almost equal amounts of water and carbon dioxide. Coal is nearly pure carbon, so for the same amount of electrical energy coal produces nearly twice as much carbon dioxide. The gas turbines we installed are 50 per cent efficient (good compared with coal stations which only convert 35 per cent of the heat energy into electricity, and lose 65 per cent as waste heat). However, if the gas were transported to small customers, such as hospitals or colleges, they could use Combined Heat and Power (CHP) and the efficiency could approach 100 per cent. This is because they could use the waste heat from the small electrical generators for space heating and other processes requiring heat, instead of sending it into the air in cooling towers. A major drawback of the policy of using gas for large-scale electricity generation is that gas reserves are low – gas will run out long before coal does.

If we are serious about reducing carbon dioxide emissions and also conserving our fuel stocks, we must think of what action we can take.

From the input side we can make use of replenishable sources of energy as much as possible, and use fossils fuels more economically as with CHP. From an output point of view, at home and work, it means better insulation and switching off unwanted appliances. Children should be encouraged to turn off lights in the school, and keep doors shut in winter. On the move it means using muscle power (walking and biking) and public transport rather than the car. Encouraging pupils to walk to school in a 'walking bus' where volunteer parents start a crocodile of children from a mile or so from the school and pick up children from their homes as the crocodile goes by, uses muscles rather than fossil fuel for transport.

The alternatives – introduction

Our way of life, which relies on fossil fuel, is not sustainable. Coal may last for 300 years, but oil and gas will run out much sooner.

What alternatives do we have? The sun provides more than enough daily energy input to supply our needs, but the problem is trapping it before it degrades as waste heat and is sent back to outer space. Only a tiny fraction of solar energy is stored through photosynthesis and climatic systems, and we would need to develop technologies which harness sunlight much more efficiently if it is to provide us with our current energy requirements (we use the word energy, here, in its fuel-value sense). Geothermal energy is a great potential source, and nuclear fusion (which mimics the processes that take place in the sun) is a hope for the future. Fusion is potentially a clean technology, producing only helium, in contrast with nuclear fission as in our present nuclear programme, whose waste products will take thousands of years to become safe, and will need secure storage.

The alternatives – a case study on biomass

Waste organic matter from life (food, crop waste, human and animal faeces, wood products etc. collectively called biomass) can be tipped (landfill), burnt (energy from waste, or from fuel crops, such as firewood), composted (as in a garden compost heap) or digested in a biogas plant (rather like what happens in a cow's stomach). These disposal systems may recover some of the minerals in the organic matter making it available to plants, and some of the fuel value (allowing us, for example, to generate electricity).

Organic material derived from oil (plastics etc.) is not biodegradable, so it can only be re-used as a feedstock for the petrochemical industry or incinerated.

Incineration

If waste organic matter from life (food, crop waste, human and animal faeces, wood products, etc.) is burnt, the minerals are recovered as ash, the carbon goes into the air as carbon dioxide, but the nitrogen is lost since it is released as nitrogen gas, which plants cannot use directly.

Biogas and land-fill gas

Food that enters a cow's (or any other animal's) gut remains a fuel until oxygen is added. Thus dried cow dung makes an excellent fuel for cooking (though the nitrogen is lost in the process) and the gases which emerge from our lower ends contain methane, which is inflammable. Digestion does not allow oxygen to join, so biomass still has fuel value. Most sewage treatment works make use of this and now digest their 'solid' sludge using anaerobic bacteria to produce methane. The remaining material, having lost much of the carbon as methane, provides a high nutrient fertiliser. The methane is burnt to fuel an electricity generator, providing power for all the pumps and often exporting power to the grid.

Similar plants in the third world provide methane gas for cooking, lighting and sometimes electricity generation to supply a village or even a homestead with clean and convenient fuel.

Composting

Composting allows aerobic bacteria to feed on the biomass, much of which is respired producing carbon dioxide. The trace elements (minerals) are all available in a useful form as compost – an excellent fertiliser and soil conditioner. If water pipes are buried in the heap, small amounts of hot water can be produced.

Summary

This chapter has dealt with different meanings of the word energy. One (measured in joules) is only known to scientists, and is a quantity that remains unaffected during changes. The other is the meaning it has in everyday language – it is what 'makes things go' and is close to the scientists' idea of a driving force, or fuel value. If energy is to be of any use to us it must be highly ordered and concentrated since as it is used it becomes spread out and scattered. You can do a lot with a red hot poker, but once its energy has been spread out into a bucket of water it is useless.

We also took a critical look at expressions such as 'food contains energy'. If food and fuel are to be a source of energy they must be combined with oxygen. The energy is stored in the fuel–oxygen system, not 'in the fuel'.

Life on Earth is driven by energy from the sun, but we have escaped from the restraints of our daily or yearly ration of sunlight, and now use 'bottled sunlight' in the form of fossil fuels (which join up with oxygen to release energy). We are using these thousands of times faster than they were made, so these reserves of fossil fuels will soon run out (gas and oil sooner than coal). Using fossil fuels also burdens the atmosphere with greenhouse gases. These two considerations suggest that we should use our energy resources as efficiently as possible, and encourage our pupils to use solar energy wherever possible. Developing 'walking buses' to school would be no bad way to start.

Chapter 7
Stardust, takeover bids and biodiversity

Liz Lakin

In this chapter we focus on life and living things. We examine the narrow margin of planet Earth that is able to support life and glimpse at its vulnerable, delicate, yet at times resilient, nature. In order to appreciate how living things function in their environment it is necessary to take a giant step back in time, back to the very beginning and explore our current understanding of how the Universe and eventually planet Earth began. Having got thus far we follow the unpredictable pathway of evolution and focus on just one of the mass extinctions experienced in the history of life on Earth. We conclude with a summary of our own evolution and the impact we are having on the planet in the short expanse of time we have existed. By considering the unpredictability of our actions, and the possible future demise of not just ourselves but many hundreds of species as well, we ask the question 'When will environmental education be taken seriously?'

By its nature this chapter covers a broad area of science and only scratches the surface of many aspects. It is designed to give an insight into the science behind one of the most fundamental of all environmental issues, that of 'living things' and our relationship with them.

Before reading further try answering these questions:

- What does the term 'biodiversity' mean to you?
- Where do you think we have come from and where are we heading?
- What is the currently agreed view of the origin of the 100 or so elements that make up the world, and how does this suggest that the Sun is a fairly recent star?
- Is it possible that we are all made of 'star dust'?
- What is the difference between a star, a planet and a moon?
- What is the connection between butterflies flapping their wings in the African jungle and a storm occurring in central London three weeks later?
- How does this relate to the early Universe, life on Earth and human impact?
- How do food chains work and why are they so important?
- Where do earthworms and fungi feature in the food chain of life?
- Does it really matter that scientists believe we are heading for the sixth mass extinction, and it is largely down to our own activities?

- What was the significance of Rio 1992?
- What can we as individuals and more specifically as teachers do to raise awareness of environmental issues?

These and other questions will be addressed in the next few pages.

Introduction

'Biodiversity is a recent concept, life on Earth a very ancient phenomenon. The history of both have fueled awareness of a global environmental crisis' (Jeffries 1997, p. 3). Modern day usage of the term 'biodiversity' combines 'the richness of life, an awareness of loss, the importance of biodiversity for economics and an ethical, social dimension' (Jeffries 1997, p. 5).

In order to gain a real appreciation for the term and its significance, it is necessary to take a closer look At the Earth, how it works and its relationship with the Solar System and the Universe.

In the beginning . . .

Our planet is just one body among many which orbit a star, our Sun – a fiery ball of hydrogen and helium gas, generating its own energy through nuclear fusion. The Sun and its orbiting planets (planets cannot generate their own energy, they rely on their sun for this), comets and meteorites comprise our Solar System, which forms a small part of a galaxy of stars; the Milky Way. There are many galaxies, with their own stars and solar systems, distributed across the Universe, but it hasn't always been like that. Fifteen billion years ago we believe things were very different.

Current scientific understanding is that the entire Universe began by being squashed up. There was a massive explosion sending out a fireball of intense heat and light, in the process creating space and time. Over the billions of years since the 'Big Bang' the energy associated with the explosion has decayed to microwaves, which are detectable in space as background radiation. These were only discovered in the early 1990s. Reiss quotes the news as it was reported in *The Independent* on 24 April 1992:

> Fourteen thousand million years ago the universe hiccuped. Yesterday, American scientists announced that they may have heard the echo. A NASA spacecraft has detected ripples at the edge of the Cosmos which are the fossilised imprint of the birth of the stars and galaxies around us today. (Reiss 1993, p. 26)

Although we do not know what triggered the explosion, our understanding of events following the 'Big Bang' has advanced over the past decade. The story is roughly as follows:

> Seconds after the Big Bang the embryonic Universe was of intense density, occupying a volume equivalent to a sphere the size of the Earth's orbit around

the Sun. The force of the explosion caused outward expansion which can still be demonstrated today by the fact that the galaxies are moving away from us. As the Universe expanded and cooled, regions of uneven and random thinning developed. This resulted in clusters of varying density. These clusters formed subatomic particles; quarks and electrons. They would be drawn towards each other by gravitational forces, yet unable to fuse owing to the excessively high temperatures.

100,000 years later the Universe had expanded further and temperatures dropped sufficiently to enable atomic nuclei to form. Protons and electrons came together to form the first atoms, hydrogen. Through a series of further nuclear fusions some helium atoms were produced. This productive stage was short-lived because temperatures continued to drop, below fusion levels, and the process was arrested. The early Universe consisted mainly of hydrogen atoms and a smaller percentage of helium.

The next three billion years saw increased activity in the newly forming Universe. Clusters of these atoms formed gas clouds unevenly distributed like islands of increased density, swirling around a central mass, rotating like 'catherine wheels'. Matter was gradually pulled inwards forming the early stars and their solar systems. These stars 'grew' in size by engulfing matter drawn towards them by increasing gravitational forces. In the biggest stars heavy elements were formed, and in the supernova death throes of the star these elements became scattered, seeding further star formation and leaving white dwarfs or black holes behind.

Children are fascinated by space and the makeup of the Universe. Being abstract, it is a difficult subject to grasp but Stannard has taken this potentially dry subject and presented it in an exciting and stimulating manner:

'Tell me something interesting, Uncle.' Gedanken lazily trailed her hand in the water.
'Something interesting?' replied Uncle Albert. He pulled the oars aboard.
'How about: You are made of stardust!'
'What does that mean? asked Gedanken
. . . Uncle Albert smiled . . . 'after the fusion, some of the stars explode'
'Explode?' . . . 'It all happens when the stars get very, very old . . . the materials thrown out of the exploding star went to form further stars – like our Sun, and the planets – like the Earth. And some was used to make people.'
'People?! Gedanken looked down at herself, and at her hands. You mean all this came out of exploding *stars*!'
'That's right – the raw materials. You're made of stardust.' (Stannard 1995, p. 59)

Primordial soup; hot springs and comet ice boxes – from chaos comes 'order'

How did life on Earth begin and from where did the raw materials originate? These questions have baffled scientists for hundreds of years, and indeed still do. Various theories have been put forward with equally varying degrees of acceptance. There are however certain 'facts' which are accepted:

- approximately 4.5 billion years ago our Sun and its nine orbiting planets (can you name them?) formed from an interstellar cloud which collapsed to make a swirling disk of gas and dust. Space debris, in the form of comets, meteorites and asteroids frequently bombarded the young planets. The ferocity of their impact on planet Earth created a hot, dry and sterile environment.

- Present day Earth has oceans and its own unique atmosphere. Scientists now believe that interstellar clouds containing gases and water molecules contributed to the makeup of our atmosphere and oceans.

- Research has revealed that terrestrial life was established enough to leave its 'calling card' in the fossil record of 3.5 billion years ago – photosynthetic bacteria found in ancient rocks from Australia and South Africa. These microfossils paint a remarkably comprehensive picture of life 3.5–3.8 billion years ago based on the synthesis of carbohydrates from carbon dioxide and water (photosynthesis). Bernstein *et al.* (1999, p. 2) suggests that for life to have been this well established in such a short geological time scale implies '. . . that the process might have required help from space molecules.' For life to have formed a series of chemical steps, as illustrated in Figure 7.1, would be necessary.

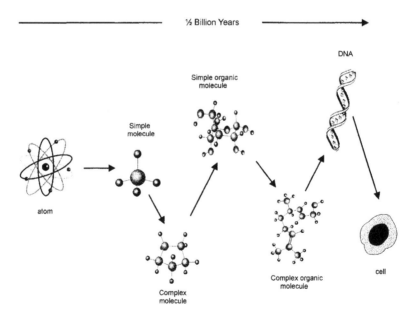

Figure 7.1 Chemical steps towards life

Stanley Miller, a graduate student in the 1950s at the University of Chicago, demonstrated how the amino acids might have originated. Simulating the early atmosphere and hostile primordial soup of pre-life Earth, Miller succeeded in synthesising these building blocks of life. Miller suggested that over real evolutionary timescales this primordial soup might have generated longer polymers capable of self-replication. (see Figure 7.2)

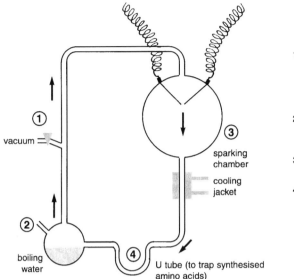

1 After the apparatus had
been evacuated, hydrogen,
ammonia & methane were
admitted at the chosen
pressures.

2 Water boiled to provide
water vapour for
oxygenation.

3 Oxidation takes place in
the sparking chamber

4 The resultant amino acids
were trapped in the U tube

Figure 7.2 Stanley Miller's experiment

There is still strong support for Miller's ideas but some scientists question the components he used in simulating the early atmosphere. There are those who visualise the event taking place on the sea floors, where murky minerals act as precursor molecules forming around the hot springs of the ocean beds. Others, for example Bernstein *et al.* (1999) look to space for assistance. They see space debris peppering the primordial soup with ready made organic molecules, kick starting the 'life forming' process. Comets (celestial iceboxes) and meteorites containing organic material in the form of amino acids and other carbon based compounds frequently bombarded the early Earth and even today we receive a rain of dust from outer space depositing an estimated three tons of organic material on Earth daily.

We often debate the idea that life could exist elsewhere in the Universe. There is still a huge gap in our understanding of how the most complex organic compounds developed into life itself, but, if molecules from space are connected with life on Earth, that means '. . . they were . . . and always are available to help with the development of life elsewhere' (Bernstein *et al.* 1999 p. 7). If indeed this is the case, what would alien life be like? This alone presents itself as an ideal topic for creative writing; art and drama!

Takeover bids and the evolution of the biosphere

Present day Earth can be viewed as a system composed of a series of interrelating components:

- *geosphere* – the Earth's physical structure comprising a crust of igneous rock, with granite forming the bulk of the continents with their mountain ranges, and basalt forming the younger oceanic basins. Below the crust is the mantle and beneath that is a core of iron.

- *atmosphere* – surrounding the planet to a distance of 160 km. Its composition is the result of physical, chemical and biological interactions taking place on the land and in the oceans since the Earth was formed (see Chapter 5), the most crucial being the evolution of the oxygen-rich atmosphere we have today.
- *hydrosphere* – about 97 per cent of the Earth's water is held in the oceans, 2 per cent frozen in glaciers and ice caps, leaving just 1 per cent as fresh water held in the ground, lakes and reservoirs. The continuous cycling of this water is vital to life on Earth.
- *biosphere* – a thin margin around the planet capable of supporting life. This region provides a mechanism for the transfer of chemicals, e.g. carbon, water, nitrates and phosphates, via a series of natural cycles.

For the Earth to have developed from a barren and lifeless planet into one displaying a great diversity of living things: plants; animals; microorganisms; viruses etc. requires, as with any self-perpetuating system, a 'feedback mechanism', essentially, a means of 'self-regulation'. Negative feedback maintains stability, positive feedback allows for progression or regression. Feedback mechanisms introduce the potential for change to arise. These in turn may bring about 'non-linear feedback' whereby the system no longer follows the establish route; a takeover bid occurs. If this results in long-term change, then evolution has taken place. Without this early Earth would have remained exactly as it was.

If systems of positive feedback became established in the primordial soup, conditions would be ripe for self-organisation and then self-perpetuation, the hallmarks of life. DNA (deoxyribose nucleic acid) is revered as the central component of cellular life, the source of commands, the instructions for replicating the species, but to make DNA you need enzymes (protein based catalysts which speed up the rate of chemical reactions in the cell) and to make enzymes, you need DNA. An evolutionary 'chicken and egg' situation. So which did come first, the enzyme or the DNA?

Questions like this have caused scientists to rethink their research and re-visit molecules they thought they understood. They now suspect that the RNA molecules (ribo-nucleic acid) played a crucial role in the evolution of life itself. Problems began on further analysis of Miller's experiment. Although ribose was present in the resulting products along with amino acids, deoxyribose (the sugar fundamental to the formation of DNA) was never found. Indeed in modern cells DNA is made from enzymes coded from RNA. A second problem arose when considering the replication process itself. This is catalysed by specific enzymes composed of long chains of amino acids. It is highly unlikely that they could have formed randomly, even given the geological timescale. It was not until the 1980s that scientists recognised the catalytical nature of RNA, enabling this molecule to act as an enzyme. These ribozymes are not very efficient but they work sufficiently well with nucleotide bases (the smallest unit from which the RNA molecule is composed) to enable copies of themselves to be made.

Stockley (1999) suggests that a small molecule of RNA, only a few bases long, but capable of catalysing simple self-perpetuation, was just what the 'pre-biotic' primordial soup needed. Trotman (1998) however, explains that self-perpetuation falls short of self-replication because it lacks precision and fidelity. What is required is an information store, replacing randomness with order. This Trotman sees as being part of a rudimentary ribosome (the cellular structure on which protein synthesis is catalysed in modern cells: see Chapter 7) forming the first accurately self-replicating entity.

So where did DNA come from?

As explained earlier, any feedback system allows for the possibility of change. The copying of information, whether using a video recorder to copy a film, or, biologically copying stored information, is prone to error. A structural change in the raw materials of replication, for example incorporating deoxyribose instead of ribose, would have been advantageous, because DNA is more robust than RNA. It results in a far more efficient and refined system. A 'takeover bid' was in place and evolution set to escalate. Once DNA was formed, simple cells followed and from these, more complex single celled organisms. The scene was set and over the next three and a half billion years new organisms appeared and disappeared, often leaving their 'calling card' in the fossil guest book. Biodiversity was set to multiply and indeed it did. Estimates of total species (the basic unit of biodiversity) alive today range between 10 and 30 million, so where have they all come from; how did they get here and why *them* and *us*?

Moths, Darwin and evolution

So many questions, but in order to make some sense of them we need to journey back in time again, back to those earliest fossil records just over three and a half billion years ago. Earth was an extremely hostile place, subject to excessive radiation and having no oxygen. The organisms alive were simply formed: bacteria, possibly some single celled plankton and much later simple multi-cellular algae, similar to *Pleurococcus* – the green powdery substance we find nowadays on the bark of trees and wooden fencing. The main difference was that all the organisms occupied the waters, there is no evidence yet for life on land, a hostile place bombarded by ultra violet light; ozone was yet to form. However, the slow production of oxygen from these photosynthetic algae ensured that the atmospere acquired its oxygen, and consequently its ozone about two billion years ago.

Things remained pretty much as they were for another billion years until changes afoot resulted in the evolution of the 'Edicarans', soft bodied creatures resembling modern day jelly fish and sea anemones, named after the Edicara Hills in South

Australia where their fossil deposits were found (Holmes 1997). Possibly also lurking in the oceans were flatworms and the early ancestors of the Arthropods.

Another thirty five million years passed with tranquil scenes of jelly fish and flatworms, until something dramatic happened in evolutionary terms. The Edicarans died out leaving only a few struggling survivors in an environment taken over by an evolutionary mega-drama – the Cambrian Explosion (see Figure 7.3).

From a history of quietly 'ticking over', evolution had woken up! Biodiversity radiated in all directions. Fossil evidence of the period comes largely from the Canadian Rocky Mountains and is labelled the 'Burgess Shale Fauna' (Holmes 1997). Consisting of tropical marine organisms, it demonstrates the widespread use of shells and other forms of exoskeleton. The biodiversity included trilobites, brachiopods, molluscs and numerous arthropods, the ancestors of modern day crabs, lobsters, woodlice and spiders. There was a marked increase in both complexity and diversity of body design, when compared with the earlier Edicarans. These newly evolved creatures possessed 'eyes' capable of seeing things, as opposed to light detectors. This created behavioural changes. Animals could now see and be seen, the predator–prey scenario had arrived, something which did not exist in the amiable waters of the Edicarans' existence.

Parker (1999) believes that this ability to make effective use of light could be the stimulus that triggered the 'evolutionary melting pot' of innovative body designs. Holmes (1997) however, looks to genetics for the answer and describes the development of a set of *hox* genes which instigate embryonic differentiation. These genes allow for differentiation of structure; the development of a head or leg, a shell or skeletal plates. Morris (1992) describes a change in climatic conditions as the possible trigger: an increase in oxygen levels and decrease in carbon dioxide; a condition that would arise with the development of more advanced photosynthetic organisms.

Regardless of what caused this evolutionary explosion, it remains clear that the outcome has not been matched at any other time in the history of life on Earth. Approximately thirty five different major groups of organisms formed, each with the potential to evolve further along their individual pathway. The interesting factor here is the unpredictable nature of what happened next. Only a limited number of organisms did evolve from that 'melting pot' and have descendants representing them today. Many died out on the way. Only those possessing the type of physiological advantage that enabled them to survive in the developing environment of early Earth, remained. One such organism was *Pikaia*, a worm-like creature, the earliest known Chordate and ancestor to the vertebrates.

Children of all ages seem fascinated by fossils and shells. They are easily found and casts can be made using plaster of Paris. Comparisons can be drawn between fossils such as *trilobites* and modern day equivalents, for example woodlice. The obscure creatures of the Burgess Shale (Gould 1990) represent a wonderful subject for creative art and modelling.

As we progress along the evolutionary pathway we meet other examples of developmental success. Populations grow and flourish, displaying clear signs of

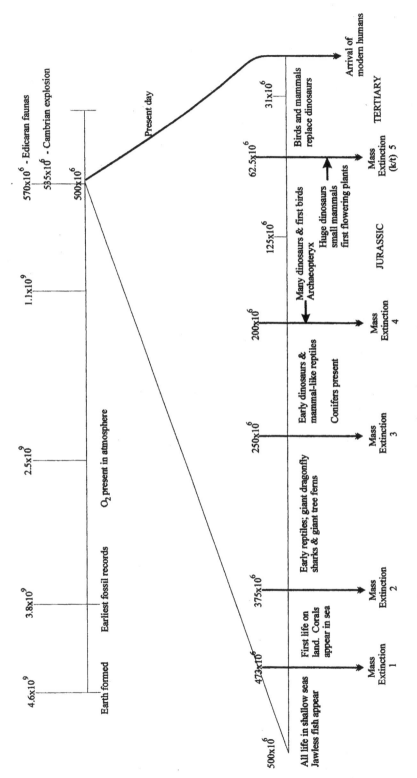

Figure 7.3 The evolution of life on Earth (measured in years from the present)

positive feedback. Stability is maintained as optimum conditions approach and negative feedback comes into play. Repeated examples are evident in Figure 7.3.

Although protected from ultra violet light for about one and a half billion years, the land mass was not colonised by life in the Devonian period until several problems were solved: organisms had to either bring the sea with them, as in land animals with tough waterproof exteriors and internal tissues bathed in blood, or do without it, as in plants with thickened cells (cellulose, lignin) for support and tubular cells for transport. Early reptiles and giant tree ferns were the dominant organisms of the Carboniferous Period. Dinosaurs flourished in the Jurassic Period and the birds, mammals and flowering plants dominated the Tertiary Period.

Why the changes? What happened to end one era and begin the next? These events are referred to as 'mass extinctions' of which five have taken place since the origins of life on Earth. The natural fate of all species is extinction, but mass extinctions do this on a grand scale. Each has resulted in a shift to a new evolutionary pathway (non-linear feedback) and proved pivotal to the history of life on Earth. Perhaps the best documented is the one responsible for the demise of the dinosaurs, sixty five million years ago. Global cooling and reduced light intensity resulting from either a comet hitting the planet or a massive volcanic eruption or both, meant that the cold-blooded dinosaurs where unable to get enough food and literally died out 'over night' in geological terms. A 'takeover' by small shrew-like mammals set the scene for the next stage in evolution; the rise of the mammals.

In spite of all the extinctions and losses, life has never been utterly destroyed. Although species diversity has generally risen over time, the majority of species that have ever lived are now extinct. Yet there are still very many species alive on Earth, so speciation (development of new species) is producing a surplus which out weighs the damage of extinction.

So what determines which direction evolution is going to take? Essentially, what an organism is like is determined by its genetic makeup and the environment in which it lives. The environment changed dramatically for the dinosaurs and they were unable to adapt, but if an organism possesses characteristics within its genetic makeup that enable it to survive in this new environment, it will. The shrew possessed a warm insulating coat of hair and maintained its body temperature above that of its surroundings, something the dinosaurs could not readily do.

Charles Darwin recognised this sequence of events in the 1800s and put forward a theory for the mechanism of evolution based on the survival of the fittest. From his studies on the Galapagos Islands and further work in the UK he published his ideas in his book *Origin of Species by Natural Selection*. Despite its hostile reception, Darwin's theory forms the basis of our understanding of evolution today. His ideas can be summarised as follows:

● adults give birth to large numbers of young;
● population sizes remain the same;

- competition exists amongst members of the population;
- all organisms within a population vary;
- some variations are more advantageous than others;
- advantageous variations will be passed on to the next generation;
- this could lead to the evolution of a new species and weed out ill-adapted members.

A modern day example of this is illustrated by *Biston Betularia* the peppered moth. It exists in two varieties; the pale, mottled or peppered form and the dark, melanic form, see Figure 7.4. The moths lived on trees covered with a pale variety of lichen. For this reason those moths which were pale in colour had an evolutionary advantage: their camouflage made them less visible to predatory birds. The darker variety was easily seen and so remained traditionally, rare. This all changed when coal used to fuel the Industrial Revolution caused deposits of soot to build up on trees in towns and cities, killing the lichen. When this happened the paler moth became more visible, whilst the melanic form gained the advantage of camouflage. Within a few generations it was the dark variety which predominated and the paler moth became the rare one.

This process of adapting to changes in the environment has been responsible for the myriad of different organisms that occupy and have occupied Earth. It is noteworthy that after a period of mass extinction there is a lack of competition which allows many variants to survive, so allowing evolutionary experimentation and speciation. This is how mammals, previously dominated and inconspicuous during the reign of the dinosaurs, were able to diversify after the mass extinction of the dinosaurs, leading to the conditions for us to evolve.

Making sense of the millions

Humans have a natural tendency to classify things and biodiversity is no exception. The biological classification system has changed over the years, depending upon what can be observed and how those observations have been interpreted. Western culture has repeatedly revised its

Figure 7.4 *Biston Betularia*, the peppered moth

understanding of the variety and nature of life on Earth:

486 BC   Greek philosopher Aristotle classified animals according to a clearly defined set of criteria recognising between 500–600 species. Modern folk classification lumped species together by broad type and recognised between 300 and 600 species

1780–1820 The Swedish biologist Linneaus developed a classification system of plants based on reproduction and of animals, based on feeding.

1800s   Nineteenth century understanding turned away from folk biology towards a biodiversity based on structure and relatedness. Cuvier pioneered comparative anatomy, particularly internal similarities as a means of classifying animals.

1900s   The twentieth century is dominated by our understanding of evolution, a theory that questions the significance of God and religion.

1950s   Whittaker's five kingdom classification was determined by advances in cell biology, enabling life to be classified according to sub-cellular features. Classification systems up to the twentieth century relied on physical, often outward appearances. Advances in technology enabled sub-cellular features to be taken into account. This new form of classification is still widely used today. (See Figure 7.5a.)

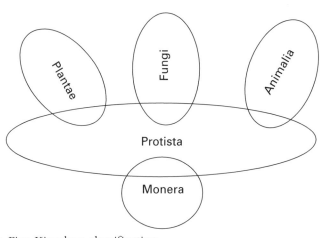

Figure 7.5a Five Kingdom classification

1990   Analysis of DNA and especially RNA suggested a fundamental revision of the classification system. This new system consists of two main branches; Bacteria on the one side and Eucarya on the other, with an early sub-division within the Eucarya branch for the Archae. A group previously believed to be closely related to the Bacteria. (See Figure 7.5b.)

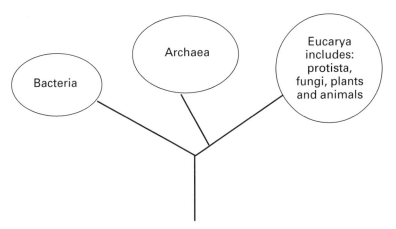

Figure 7.5b Three domain revision

Getting the connection (ecosystems)

All these organisms live within their environment responding over the years to the various changes that take place. To fully appreciate the significance of environmental change there is a need to understand how the environment works. This is best achieved by exploring a typical ecosystem; a biological community of interacting organisms and their physical environment. Jeffries (1997) explains that the activity of natural ecosystems provides what are now called services or functions vital to a healthy planet. Let us consider a deciduous woodland ecosystem. Picture an ancient oak with its myriad of organisms living on and feeding off it. The oak produces acorns and leaves, bark and wood, for its own benefit but also of vital importance to several other organisms including the winter moth caterpillar munching at its leaves. Nestled further up in the branches sits a blue tit with several hungry young. In the distance is the cry of sparrowhawk fledglings impatiently awaiting their next meal. At the foot of the tree in amongst last autumn's leaf litter, an earthworm pulls a leaf into its burrow and woodlice busy themselves nibbling at broken twigs. A rare toadstool pokes its cap through the damp mulch reaching for the air above.

This familiar scene captures all aspects of a thriving ecosystem, driven by the transfer of energy from the Sun and enriched by the nutrients recycled in the soil. Yet as with most energy transfer systems, it is inefficient due to the many losses in the system. Of all the light from the sun falling on the planet, only 5 per cent is available for use by green plants and other autotrophs during photosynthesis. Of this only a small percentage is used for growth and building up biomass. It is this which is transferred to the consumer, in this case the Winter Moth caterpillar. The caterpillar must use the energy released during respiration of this biomass to carry out its metabolic functions, including respiration itself. Only 10 per cent is assimilated, being used for growth, repair and reproduction. The blue tit young being fed the caterpillar, and the sparrowhawk fledgling, being fed the blue tit young, will benefit from an even smaller percentage. Food chains like this emphasise how the energy transfer system limits the total amount of biomass available and the number of organisms able to survive at the top of the food chain. Chains such as these do not work in isolation; associated with our oak tree are many such food chains interlinking to form one interdependent food web.

'Timing' is vital. For the system to remain in balance and be sustainable, all players, whether biological or physical, have their role to play and a narrow window of time in which to act. If the oak trees leaves opened too early due to an exceptionally warm spring, by the time the winter moth caterpillar was ready to eat them they would be old, tough and full of toxins. If the leaves opened too late possibly because of low light intensities brought on by increased air pollution, the leaves would not be available for the caterpillar. In either scenario, the caterpillar population would suffer, which would have similar effects on both the blue tit and sparrowhawk young.

Energy transfer may be inefficient, but nutrient recycling is crucial. Inorganic chemicals such as nitrogen, magnesium, phosphorus etc. required to sustain the system, are finite. Once they are taken out of the soil by the plant they have to pass through a biomass pool and then a decay pool, before being returned to the soil as inorganic chemicals again. Earthworms, woodlice fungi and bacteria are

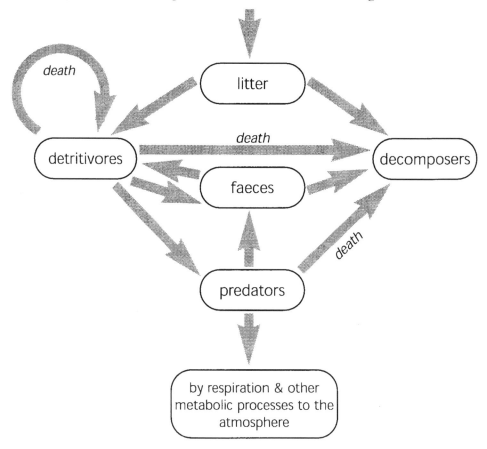

Figure 7.6 Flows of energy in the decomposition of leaf litter

responsible for this. Without them the system would break down. (See Figure 7.6.)

Jones (1997) explains that bottlenecks occur naturally in ecosystems where nutrients get held in one pool for too long. In tropical rainforests 'nutrients are locked up in the tree trunk, in the open sea most nutrients are in the dark, deeper reaches where photosynthesis cannot occur, and in peat bogs most nutrients are locked in dead, but not decomposed, organic matter' (Jones 1997, p. 12).

Similar bottlenecks occur when a field is harvested. The crop takes up nutrients as it builds up biomass. By harvesting the crop, the nutrients are removed from the soil and from that particular ecosystem. The soil becomes thin and infertile and blows away. The system begins to run down. This is why farmers have to use fertilisers (e.g. by composting waste from food so that the nutrients are returned to the soil in that way).

Human impact

Ecosystems are self-sufficient environments, but at the same time vulnerable to change and exploitation. It has become increasingly evident over the past decade that the human race is having a profound effect on these natural environments and their physical and biological components (IPCC 1995).

The interesting and indeed profoundly concerning fact about this impact is the unpredictable nature of its outcome. Polkinghorne (1999) explains that the world does have some clocks in it, things which behave in a regular fashion, that are reliable and very predictable. There are however, exceptions 'Systems that are so exquisitely sensitive that the slightest disturbance will totally change their future behaviour' (p.3). This is called the 'Butterfly Effect' and it applies equally to the evolution of the Universe and planet Earth, our inability to make long range weather forecasts and to the outcome of our everyday activities when combined with the instability of the natural cycles that sustain the planet. The scale and magnitude of our impact on the environment is well documented, but only the major areas for concern are highlighted below.

Climate change and the carbon cycle

On the 11th August 1999 not only was the sun obscured from view during the 'Last Eclipse' of the 20th century, but as reported by *The Independent* (1999) newspaper 'The National Grid' had its biggest power surge. As people returned to work they produced a massive surge of 3,000 megawatts. There was a sudden demand for electricity, as computers, lights and other electrical appliances were switched back on. This was equivalent to the electrical output of three large power stations. Records were broken in January 1995 when the standard pull on the Grid reached 50,000 megawatts. This scale of demand illustrates the direction in which the western worlds reliance on electricity is heading. It is, however, unsustainable. Current figures for sources of electricity generation in the UK (DTI

1998) indicate that coal still held the largest share of the market in 1997, with nuclear and gas a close second and third. These three main suppliers have jockeyed for prime position continuously over the last few years but with the political, economic and controversial nature of electricity generation the future looks set to be a greater coal burn.

Replenishable supplies such as solar, wind and hydro will have their role to play but only via small, possibly localised generation schemes. Coal has the potential to meet our ever increasing demand for electricity well into the next millennium, but the impact of burning fossil fuels, whether in power stations or in our cars, has set 'alarm bells ringing' among environmentalists and governments alike, since the early 1970s. Carbon dioxide, the most anthropogenic greenhouse gas (see Chapter 5), is produced during the combustion of fossil fuels. Carbon, locked up as 'coal' from the fossilised remains of Jurassic and Carboniferous forests, is released once more into the atmosphere to play an active role in the carbon cycle. This may not seem a problem until we recognise that our increased use of such fuels is contributing to the exaggerated greenhouse effect and global warming (IPCC 1992). The long-term implications on the global ecosystem are uncertain, but indications point to the following:

> sea level rise resulting from icecaps melting and thermal expansion of the seas;
> flooding in low lying areas of the world e.g. the Netherlands and Bangladesh;
> some low lying islands, for example in the Pacific, could disappear;
> unpredictable extremes of climate conditions;
> disruption to crop growing as climate patterns change. (Elliott 1997, pp. 26–8)

Burning of fossil fuels serves to enhance the problem, another contributor is the large scale 'deforestation' which removes the natural 'sink' for carbon.

Forests and deforestation

Forests cover 34 per cent of the world's surface and contain as much as 90 per cent of all terrestrial species of plants and animals. Howard (1998) explains that they regulate global climate, prevent soil erosion and protect watersheds. They are a major source of medicinal plants and support a global trade in pulp and timber, sustaining 2 per cent of world trade. The main reasons for felling are twofold:

- wood and wood pulp consumption, whereby 5 per cent of the world are responsible for 80 per cent of consumption. In the UK alone 50 million cubic metres of timber and paper pulp are consumed each year and 4 million tons of timber end up in land fill sites!
- clearance for cash crop plantations e.g. tea; coffee; oil palm and pineapple for exportation.

Howard (1998) explains that for decades the destruction of the world's forests has been recognised as one of the biggest environmental problems of our time resulting in widespread fragmentation of ecosystems and endangering many species.

This type of damage incurred to nature by humans, is seldom driven by destructive spite, but due to human pressures of population growth, culture, institutional and economic failure (Jeffries 1997). The latter has been cited as fundamental to forest exploitation in many developing countries, as these natural resources have been used to generate the foreign exchange required to meet debt repayments (Howard 1998).

Endangered species and the alien crayfish

Cultural traditions, beliefs and customs have much to answer for when we consider the demise of several species. Traditional medicine has pushed the Sumatran rhino to the brink of extinction; processed rhino horn can command £1000 per ounce for use in Chinese medicine. Similarly, the male harp seals, which have been heavily culled for the medicinal use of their penises. The demand for exotically coloured pearls has pushed one species of mussel close to extinction because its shell can be ground up and fed to oysters, colouring the pearls they produce. Our own insatiable demand for fish and chips has left cod and haddock populations facing near extinctions within three years unless radical measures are taken.

Competition from introduced species has had similar effects. New species are deliberately introduced for a variety of reasons, sometimes genuinely because it is felt that the new species will solve an ecological problem. Problems with introducing alien species are that they can escape into the wild and create problems with the natives. This is all too evident with the case of the signal crayfish from North America (Figure 7.7) which were introduced into English waters in the mid 1970s in response to a demise in the native white clawed variety at a time when crayfish were developing as a culinary luxury in Western Europe. The American version was hardy, fast growing, aggressive and it harboured the fungal infection responsible for crayfish plague. Many escaped from captivity, establishing populations in the wild. The native white claw was susceptible to crayfish plague and fell foul of the infection, reducing their populations even further. The story, unfortunately, does not end there. The white clawed crayfish is described by ecologists as a 'keystone species' – one on which the numbers of many other species are supported or held in balance (Holdich 1994). The demise of one such population has serious and detrimental effects on a host of others.

Fertiliser, the nitrogen cycle and eutrophication

As human populations increase, so too do the pressures on farmers to get the most out of their soil. Nitrogen is a vital element for all living things because it is fundamental to the structure of proteins and nucleic acids. As it is such a significant element it can be appreciated why farmers are so keen to maintain its levels in their soil. As plants grow they remove nitrogen as minerals dissolved in water in the soil by their roots. In a natural situation this would be recycled over a period of time and the system would be maintained in a dynamic equilibrium.

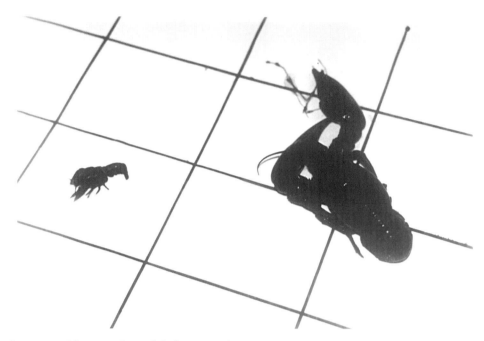

Figure 7.7 The signal crayfish from North America

In the past, when the land lost its fertility through frequent cropping, people would move on to new land. This is still done in parts of the world where land is cleared by 'slash and burn' and cultivated for a few years then allowed to revert back to jungle. Once farmers settled permanently in one place they would allow a field to lie fallow for a year after several years cropping. This would allow the soil to regain its fertility.

Farming has altered over the decades to accommodate an increasing demand for food. Fields now exist as monocultures – a single crop being intensively farmed (see Chapter 8). This puts a tremendous pressure on the soil and its nitrogen content. To compensate, farmers use nitrogen-rich fertilisers, enabling them to produce high quality plants at high yields from increasingly depleted soils.

Heavy rainfall washes some of the fertiliser into nearby rivers because it is water soluble, causing nitrogen levels to increase and plant life to blossom. This nutrient-rich condition is referred to as 'eutrophication'. The effects can be devastating. In the daytime plants photosynthesise, releasing oxygen. This will support increasing populations of animals. During the night, when photo-synthesis ceases, both plant and animal populations compete for the available oxygen for respiration. This competition results in fatalities which increases the population of decomposing bacteria using the dead organic material as food. The bacteria require oxygen as well for respiration. This example of positive feedback results in a collapsed ecosystem resulting from long-term depletion of oxygen. Pastoral farming can have a similar effect resulting from the leaching of cattle, sheep and pig manure and urine from soils and into water courses.

These examples are windows into a world that is dominated by humans. We have as much right to be here as any one of the organisms described in the earlier sections of this chapter, yet we appear to have made far more of a mark on the planet in the short expanse of time that we have existed, than any other species. One could put the question 'Does it matter? We are part of nature and therefore only doing what is natural!' In a way that's true, we *are* part of nature and we are developing and using the greatest asset we have been given – our brain. Life on Earth is a history of extinctions, so why should we worry that the biodiversity of Earth is decreasing today, largely due to human activity? One asset that our advanced brain has is the sense of 'forethought' and the ability to predict ahead. Even into a seemingly unpredictable environment we are able to model possible outcomes and guess at possible future scenarios. These are what we need to take heed of.

So where do we go from here and what can be done?

In 1992, 179 different governments were represented at the Earth Summit which took place in Rio de Janeiro. The Summit was the product of global environmental concerns which began in the 1970s. Various other developments led to the conference in Rio in 1992, the aim of which was to produce a document outlining how the various governments would take more care of the environment. The biggest challenge was for them all to agree to it and then act upon it. The document was entitled 'Agenda 21' – a common agenda for the 21st century agreed to by all 179 different governments. It set out policies and action plans for countries to address the major environmental issues, such as carbon dioxide emissions and global warming, waste minimisation, biodiversity and the loss of habitat and species, natural disasters and above all else the notion of sustainability: 'meeting the needs of the present without compromising the ability of the future generations to meet their needs' (Peace Child International 1994, p. 6).

Agenda 21 was definitely a step in the right direction but as with the outcomes of many conferences, the delegates go home and reality hits them. Many countries worked towards the agenda but some seven years down the road, we still have a great deal to do. Government legislation has come and gone and the pressures on the planet are still as real and concerning as ever. It all comes down to our willingness and potential to take effective action. In order to do this we, as individual nations, need to have commitment on a political, social and economic scale. This is not so easy to achieve. As individual people however, we need to be fully aware of the environmental issues and the science behind them. This is achievable and much can be done to reach this. The government sponsored 'Going for Green' campaign is aimed at raising awareness amongst individuals (including children), action groups and businesses. The campaign involves a clearly defined code of good practice, a millennium pledge, environmental 'theme a month' with suggested activities for all to be involved with. Other initiatives include the Tidy Britain Groups involvement with the 'Children's

Parliament', involving children in the major issues of improving the environment. The Environment Agency has also been proactive in raising awareness by producing literature and their *Environment Action*; a bi-monthly newspaper outlining environment related activities nationwide.

These resources and initiatives work, but at a superficial level. In the classroom environment awareness and appreciation of our own impact on the environment should be fundamental to teaching and learning:

- As well as having daily monitors for administration purposes, have a light monitor, a child responsible for 'switching it off'! when the lights are not required (see Chapter 6).
- Ensure paper is reused and overall usage reduced (think of the 4 million tons in the land fill sites!) (see Chapter 5).
- Think about waste generally and the impact of packaging on the environment (see Chapters 3 and 5).
- Encourage the children to learn more about their local environment and the influences on it. This introduces not only the physical but also the biological environment, developing a sense of caring and ownership. Ideas leading to conservation and sustainability can be developed from this (see Chapter 4).
- The importance of water and other natural resources can form the basis of several science and environmental sessions (see Chapter 5).
- Encourage the children to think environmentally outside of school. Nowadays most children have access to a television, if not one of their own! How many leave these and other electronic equipment on 'standby'? This uses electricity, wasting in total the equivalent of a quarter of a large power station's capacity. This has financial implications as well as depleting non-replenishable natural resources. These reasons for 'switching it off'! may not mean much initially to the children, but if you explain that the majority of household fires are caused by equipment left on 'standby', the message soon gets home (see Chapter 6).

Summary

During this chapter we have explored the history of life on Earth. We began with the unstructured beginnings of the Big Bang, the evolution of the Universe, our Solar System and the development of early Earth. We touched on several theories of how life began, visited its evolutionary infancy and its racy 'teenage' experimentations in the Cambrian period. Over the four billion years of its history we saw biodiversity wax and wane with some catastrophic extinction events bringing in periods of rapid evolutionary change. During this time span, Earth has developed from a barren and lifeless entity to a highly ordered, self-sustaining system. Yet activities which have taken place over the last few thousand years threaten that order and sustainability, bringing to question the future of the planet and more specifically the species responsible for damaging the system – us!

It is by no means clear how the future may unfold owing to the unpredictable nature of the situation, but as humans we have the ability to model a range of possible scenarios based on the facts available now. Warning signs have already been recognised and we must decide as individuals as to whether or not we are prepared to respond.

A final thought:

The principles and practice of good conservation are well understood throughout the world. The real challenge is whether we can be bothered. Ultimately conservation is not about the details of genetics, zoo management or treaty clauses. Conservation depends on our commitment. (Jeffries 1997, p. 181)

Chapter 8

Farming, food and feeding the world

Liz Lakin

The results of a survey conducted on behalf of the National Farmers (1997) indicate an alarming lack of knowledge amongst 8–11 year olds about food and farming. Of the 250 pupils interviewed findings indicated:

- 50 per cent of the children thought margarine was produced from cows milk;
- 33 per cent thought oranges were grown in Britain;
- 50 per cent thought that spinach was grown abroad;
- 10 per cent did not know that ham came from a pig;
- 25 per cent did not know that bread is made from wheat.

In this chapter we will look at the history of farming and how it has impacted on our lives. We will project forward into an unknown future where the struggle for food and water could be the driving force of political and international conflict. By exploring several possible strategies for addressing this global food crisis, we discuss biotechnology and genetic engineering and its potential impact. This raises issues of awareness and education. The chapter concludes by looking back at the above survey results and emphasising the need for sound food education at all levels.

To achieve this we must first begin with the basis of food production – the 'plant', and work our way up from there.

Plants and how they work

Consider these questions and how children may respond to them:

- Why do daffodils produce flowers?
- Why do apple trees produce apples?

Children tend to answer the first by saying 'they look pretty'. In the same way, apples are for us to eat. It takes children a while to realise that flowers on plants produce fruits which contain the seeds to allow them to reproduce. The flower forms the reproductive structure of the plant (see Figure 8.1).

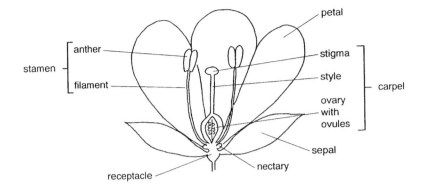

*Generalised section through an insect
pollinated flower*

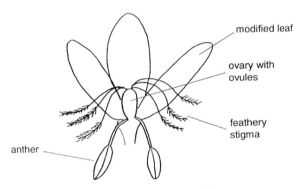

*Generalised section through a wind
pollinated flower (eg grasses)*

Figure 8.1 Reproductive structures in two kinds of plant

You will see that different flowers vary considerably in their structure. Some are relatively simple, e.g. celandine and buttercup, while others are more complex, e.g. runner bean, white dead nettles or honeysuckle. Some flowers are really collections of flowers (an inflorescence), such as the sunflower, dandelion or cow parsley. Cultivated flowers are often heavily changed by artificial selection, making it difficult to recognise their parts. Flowers that are pollinated by insects are brightly coloured with sugary nectar and attractive scents to entice the local insects. Flowers that are pollinated by wind are inconspicuous (grasses), produce large amounts of pollen and often have feathery styles to catch the pollen from the wind.

Usually the pollen must be transferred to another flower for cross pollination to take place so the seed can grow. The flower is pollinated when pollen grains (containing male sex cells) land on the stigma of the carpel. A pollen tube grows to the ovule (containing the female sex cells). The male and female sex cells fuse (fertilisation) and over a period of time develop into the seed. This becomes encased in a fruit which assists the dispersal of the seed. Fruits vary both in design and makeup, but their main role is to ensure that the seed is removed as far away as possible from the parent plant.

The seed is essentially an embryonic new plant, equipped with its own food supply. When the seed is warm and wet, this food supply becomes mobilised and the seed germinates. This food supply acts as raw material for early growth, but also as a fuel supply enabling metabolism to take place. This means that the seed needs access to oxygen.

The root (radical) grows first and takes in water. The shoot (plumule) develops and when it reaches the light the first green leaves photosynthesise. Once this stage has been reached the seedling can now put its energies into building up biomass; it begins to grow.

Now consider where the materials come from for a plant to grow, (Figure 8.2).

Most children and adults pay more attention to the water and soil as a source of materials and omit substances from the air, but plants need water, carbon dioxide and minerals to grow. Plants make up their structure (biomass) mainly from the products of photosynthesis. This process involves water, carbon dioxide and sunlight energy in the presence of the green pigment 'chlorophyll'. This produces free oxygen and carbohydrate which is further converted with important mineral additions to produce biomass. During respiration the energy stored from photosynthesis is released when the biomass is rejoined with oxygen. Biomass can be seen as both a building material for plants and a fuel for respiration (see Chapter 6).

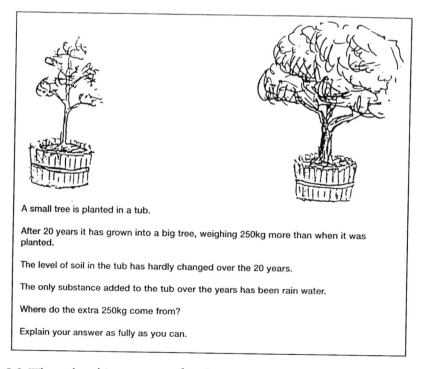

A small tree is planted in a tub.

After 20 years it has grown into a big tree, weighing 250kg more than when it was planted.

The level of soil in the tub has hardly changed over the 20 years.

The only substance added to the tub over the years has been rain water.

Where do the extra 250kg come from?

Explain your answer as fully as you can.

Figure 8.2 Where does biomass come from?

We now consider these small, but essential mineral additions which most plants obtain from quality soil.

Muck and mystery (about the soil)

Soils can vary in colour and texture, depending upon the base rock from which they are formed. But it is the organic matter and plant cover that allows these broken bits of rock to remain fixed to the ground. You only need to look at the devastation of heavy rain on unprotected fields or cleared forests to see how the plant cover binds and protects the soil. In coastal areas grasses are planted on sand dunes to stabilise them and prevent erosion from the wind.

Soil provides anchorage for plants, but it also supplies water, air and minerals to the roots of plants. The minerals are ionic inorganic substances dissolved in the water (see Figure 8.3). Both minerals and water are carried to the leaves where they play a crucial role in plant metabolism. The process begins with

The Inorganic Elements

Major elements:

Nitrogen(N)	As nitrates or ammonium salts	Essential part of proteins in plants	Fertilisers normally contain all or some of these plant nutrients.
Phophorus (P)	As phosphate salts	Essential for photosynthesis	May be natural or manufactured in origin
Potassium (K)	In salts	Resist disease and help transport nutrients	

Secondary elements (as ions):

Sulphur (S)	As sulphate salts	
Magnesium (Mg)		These may need to be added from time to time
Calcium (Ca)		
Sodium (Na)	Especially for beet crops	

Trace elements (as ions):

Iron (Fe)		These are normally present in the soil in the small amounts plants need. They are easily added if needed
Boron (B)		
Manganese (Mn)		
Molybdenum (Mo)		
Zinc (Zn)		
Cobalt (Co)		
Copper (Cu)		

Figure 8.3 Elements for plant metabolism

photosynthesis producing carbohydrates. These are distributed around the plant, providing fuel for respiration and, together with the minerals, materials for growth. Oxygen is obtained from the atmosphere and from air trapped within the soil structure.

But this is not all. The soil contains fungi, microbes, and small animals. These feed off dead organisms and, through their excretion products, help plants obtain the minerals they need. This relationship is fundamental to the recycling of these finite nutrients that sustain living things.

Children tend to think of soil as 'dirt' that always remains in one place and is uniform throughout. By encouraging children to explore soil and the myriad of organisms that inhabit it, they can develop an understanding of its structure and composition and the vital role it has to play in the giant food web of life.

History of farming

Fossil evidence indicates that humans evolved from tree-dwelling apes, feeding mainly off fruits and seeds. Somewhere between 10 and 4 million years ago climatic change forced these apes to move down to the ground and they supplemented this herbivorous diet with bark, shoots, small insects, lizards and frogs. They had become omnivorous. Other features developed which are apparent in the fossil record:

- sharp eyes to find fruit and small creatures;
- manual dexterity to pluck fruit and pick up small insects;
- ability to digest protein;
- size of the teeth reduced as transition from human-like ape to ape-like human took place, (this reduction in teeth and jaw size continues even today, as a consequence of the introduction of cooking);
- progression to an upright stance as our ancestors developed the ability to hunt and kill;
- the use of fire and the development of tools (evidence of Peking Man, approximately 500,000 years ago, a cave dweller known to have used fire and fed mainly off venison);
- development of fish hooks (approximately 25,000 years ago) dug out canoes and rafts first made their appearance approximately 10,000 years ago.

Further climate change, together with the effects of hunting, caused the fauna to change and habits altered yet again. The hunters found that they could entice animals to come to them by providing food, and the gatherers began to live near their plant food supply, ready for harvest. This was a slow process happening at different times in different parts of the world. Evidence suggests that by about 9000 BC small settlements were developing consisting of hunters and intensive gathering of plant food material from the local environment. Burning, clearing and cultivation took place and by 5000 BC, the Neolithic times, widespread forest clearance took place to provide space for cultivation. The areas were farmed until the soil was depleted of minerals and yields had reduced.

Settlements would be abandoned and the people moved to new areas. The whole process was then repeated. This practice of shifting cultivation still continues today in many parts of the world.

The Iron and Bronze ages saw more developments and population increases. This put greater demand on food supply. Domestication of plants took place, followed by that of animals. The first animals to be domesticated were dogs. These supplemented the hunters skills and were also used for herding. A compromise had to be made between the farming of grazing animals for their meat and other products, and their threat to the yield of grain crop.

Up to the period historians refer to as the 'Dark Ages' in Europe, approximately 1500 years ago, farming centred around crops. At around 500 AD there was a dramatic change in climate, resulting in reduced light and harsh, cold conditions. The crops failed and many people died from starvation, cold conditions and diseases such as the 'Black Death'. Those who did survive looked for alternative food supplies, resulting in different farming practices. In the UK sheep farming developed, revolutionising the use and ownership of land. For the next two hundred and fifty years farming developed in tune with the increasing population. Crop plants had returned, with wheat, the most important. The use of animals for food was still limited to goats and sheep, domestication of pigs came later. Finally came cattle but only the most docile could be caught and contained. Once domesticated they provided a variety of commodities ranging from food to skins/hides for watertight containers and clothing, to dung for fuel. They were also used to tread in seeds and pull ploughs.

By choosing the best animals and crops for breeding, humans could ensure future productivity. Selective breeding began thousands of years ago, in Egypt, providing the basis for modern breeding programmes focusing on producing food for an ever increasing population.

By the turn of the twentieth century knowledge of the reproductive processes and the genetics of crop plants and domesticated animals was developing. This brought improvements in the quality and availability of food, leading to the 'intensive farming' era.

The advent of intensive farming

The 1947 Agricultural Act, supported by the UK government and European policy, had as its key objective to increase agricultural production and achieve self-sufficiency in basic foodstuffs such as milk, cereal and beef. To ensure this the following measures were implemented:

- Guaranteed prices: Farmers were offered a guaranteed price for the basic foodstuffs, maintained by the government.
- Grants and subsidies: These were made available to increase the efficiency of farms, by enabling the farmer to buy machinery and fertilisers. Mechanisation and intensification were actively encouraged.

When Britain joined the EEC in 1973, farmers still continued to benefit from guaranteed prices, grants and subsidies under the Common Agricultural Policy (CAP). CAP protected European farmers by placing levies on imported products and by buying up surplus stocks, thereby protecting the farmers income. This led to the notorious grain mountains and milk lakes of the 1970s.

By the early 1980s it had become evident that forty years of intensive farming was taking its toll on the countryside. Interest groups lobbied Parliament and by 1992 the government cut the guaranteed price for cereals and livestock. At the same time several environmental measures where introduced which included:

- Set-aside
- Nitrogen Sensitive Areas
- Environmentally Sensitive Areas
- Countryside Stewardship Schemes
- Hedgerow Incentives
- New Habitat Schemes
- Organic Initiatives

Agricultural production was reduced and with it, environmental impact. This, however saw the beginning of the demise of the UK farming industry, at a time when food for the future was becoming an issue.

Food for the 21st century

Within forty five years the demand for food on a global scale is set to triple. Within just thirty years the world's population is expected to grow by nearly half, from 5.7 billion to about 8.5 billion people – all of whom will require feeding. MacMillain (1996) suggests that this increasing population will be demanding higher-value food products in the form of animal protein. This will be reflected in a global market pull for such products and their associated production crops: feed grains and oilseeds. This is already apparent in such countries as China and India who are experiencing an economic growth of six per cent per year.

Eating continually at the highest level of the food chain (see Chapter 7) is not sustainable. Approximately 20 kg of grain are required to produce 1 kg of meat. Conner (1997) argues that this is not efficient use of the land available for food production and states that we, in the Western World, should be adopting more of a vegetarian diet. His reasons focus on the efficiency of food production and he cites the connections between diet and heart disease.

If we consider the global amount of agricultural land available and take into account predictions concerning the future use of land for electricity generation, it is postulated that 14 million hectares in Europe alone will be turned over to biomass for fuel production in the next fifteen years. This will provide a fuel source for power stations and meet the increasing demand for electricity from replenishable energy sources. If, as suggested, this land will come from existing agricultural land, where will the food come from?

MacMillain (1996) advocates better land management, to ensure more effective use of the land available. He claims that farmers across the globe require a greater knowledge of the advances in modern biotechnology and agrochemicals. In order to gain maximum productivity from their land, the knowledge of seed varieties, fertiliser and chemicals suitable for their specific circumstances needs to be accessible, together with production and management techniques. Herbivores, such as cattle, pigs and sheep need to be kept within the carrying capacity of the ecosystem (see Chapter 7) and overall biodiversity needs to be maintained. MacMillain (1999) also believes that current advances in biotechnology could hold the key to future productivity.

Biotechnology

Biotechnology, that area of science by which we manipulate biological organisms, systems or processes for our own benefit, in agriculture, food production and medicine, has been practised for thousands of years.

Early humans noticed the variations in living organisms and started to use it to their advantage. Farmers selected seeds from plants with the heaviest yields to grow next year's crops; others selected bull calves from cows that produced high milk yields to sire the next generation of calves. This process has continued throughout the course of human history. Farmers have selected features from decades of farm horses to produce the 'shire', a placid animal, yet immensely strong. Broiler chickens have been selected to meet the demands of life style changes; in two generations poultry meat has gone from being a luxury to becoming the cheapest of all high-protein foods. Modern day chickens grow three times faster and have six to seven times more meat than their counterparts fifty years ago.

A more recent development, illustrating traditional techniques of selection is the 'Cotswold Diamond'. Breeding experts crossed an American red-haired Duroc pig with the British Landrace, selecting the most sociable animals and breeding out the Durocs course red hair. The pork and bacon from the offspring is lean and the pigs are more tolerant of each other; a characteristic worth developing as new welfare laws introduced in 1999 made tethering in single pens illegal, a traditional practice which kept grumpy, often aggressive pigs apart.

Cross-breeding, however, does present its problems owing to the complex relationship between genetic make-up (genotype) and physical make-up (phenotype). Unwanted combinations of genes can arise, with alarming outcomes: chickens with a very high egg production capacity obtained the extra calcium needed for shells at the expense of their bones, resulting in the onset of osteoporosis. High yielding dairy cattle deformed beneath the weight of their milk often suffer from arthritis. The international dog show, Crufts, provides examples of extremes that have been reached: the champion boxers that can no longer feed themselves and the array of breeds which are so far removed from the ancestral 'dog' it is difficult to see the relationship.

Quicker than evolution, traditional methods of selective breeding are still employed in breeding programmes across the globe, but they are much slower than the most recent biotechnological technique: one of which is never far from the spotlights of everyday journalism – *genetic engineering.*

It's all in the genes

In order to get a feel for what genetic engineering is and how it works, it is necessary to understand something about *genes.* Try answering these four questions:

- What are genes and whereabouts are yours?
- Do bacteria have genes?
- Is the information in the sex cells the same as in the other cells of your body?
- What is the difference between Polly and Dolly?

These are answered in the sections which follow.

The work of Gregor Mendel, a nineteenth century Austrian monk whose interest in heredity and breeding fathered the area of science known as 'genetics', demonstrated that characteristics of living organisms are inherited from one generation to the next. Approximately fifty years ago the scientists Watson and Crick along with others discovered that the information which determines these characteristics was contained in a molecule called deoxyribonucleic acid (DNA). This molecule is arranged into segments known as genes which are themselves organised into structures called chromosomes. All organisms, including bacteria have chromosomes, although the number and location within the cell is dependent upon the type of organism. Bacteria contain a single chromosome floating freely within the cell. The majority of other organisms contain a nucleus within their cells and the chromosomes are located there. They become visible when the cell is dividing.

The DNA present within all organisms is identical in the manner it carries the information for specific characteristics. Yet we know that all organisms vary! Even within our own families there are striking differences between individuals. It is this idea of variation that is fundamental to genetics and the various fields of science that have emerged from it.

The genetic code

In order to understand the essence of variation and how this phenomenon is explained by modern genetics, we need to understand the nature and structure of DNA. The backbone of the molecule consists of alternating sugar–phosphate linkages and attached to each linkage is a base (see Figure 8.4). There are four types of bases: adenine (A), cytosine (C), guanine (G) and thymine (T), which pair up A–T and G–C to form the rungs of the spiral. The whole structure is wound into a double helix which forms the chromosome.

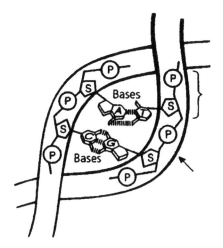

Figure 8.4 A DNA molecule

The genes on the chromosome contain information in the form of the 'genetic code', derived from the order in which the bases are arranged. The sequence of bases on the genes govern the sequence of building blocks (amino acids) that make up the proteins; the primary constituent of living things. In this way, DNA determines the characteristics of the organism. The process by which DNA encodes the structure of proteins is known as the 'genetic code'. This is translated and interpreted by a similar molecule, called RNA, as part of the process for the manufacture of proteins which make up the structure of enzymes. Enzymes are centrally important chemicals which control all cellular reactions in the body; in this way the DNA code controls body activities.

Variation and natural selection

The DNA making up the gene for a certain characteristic may itself vary, both within individuals and within a population. For example, the gene for eye colour pigment can vary so that some eyes are brown, while others are blue, green or some other colour. Differences in DNA cause variations in organisms (see Chapter 7).

Differences in the DNA do not only affect appearances. They can affect the quality of a crop, for example:

- increasing the amount of starch in potatoes;
- improving the resistance of oilseed rape to herbicides;
- enabling tomatoes to remain fresher for longer.

New variations are caused by changes to the DNA and these changes are called 'mutations'. In nature, variations in the DNA of organisms means that some individuals are better adapted than others to live under particular environmental conditions. The result of this is that better-adapted individuals out-compete their neighbours and are more likely to reproduce, passing their successful genes to the next generation. 'Nature' is selecting those organisms most likely to flourish. This gives rise to the term 'natural selection', which is explored in more detail in Chapter 7. In this way the make-up of an animal or plant population slowly changes with time as the organism becomes more adapted to the environment in which it lives. Over the centuries we have exploited this 'natural process', taking natures role as the selector and driving the process in a direction that benefits us. The story of 'wheat' illustrates this clearly.

Case study 4: wheat

Ask a child what bread is made from and they will probably say 'flour'; ask them the same question about pasta and the reply is invariably 'out of a packet'. Our general knowledge of wheat, the basic ingredient of both bread and pasta, is very limited, yet it is a crop which forms the staple diet of more than a third of the world's population. Possibly the first crop to be grown by humans, its history can be traced back 10,000 years. Yet modern day wheat is very different from its ancestral type, *Triticum monococcum* or einkorn wheat. The most striking variation occurs within the cells, the chromosome number. Modern day wheat has three times as many chromosomes per cell as the wild version which only contains fourteen. The occurrence of multiple sets of chromosomes is rare in animals but fundamental to plant evolution. Almost 50 per cent of all known species of flowering plants display this phenomenon called 'Polyploidy'. This is the occurrence of multiple sets of chromosomes resulting from unequal cell division and chromosome doubling. The chromosomes have replicated and divided, yet the nucleus fails to divide resulting in a cell with double the total number of chromosomes.

In a normal cell the total number of chromosomes is referred to as the diploid number or *2n*. In the sex cells, for example egg, or sperm cells, only half the chromosomes are present, the chromosome number is now *n* and termed haploid. On fertilisation the diploid number is regained. In polyploidy, doubling of the chromosome number results in a tetraploid cell where the number of chromosomes is *4n*. A genetic cross between a diploid plant and a tetraploid plant would result in a *3n* triploid hybrid. Polyploidy occurs spontaneously in many plants, each resuming normal division the next time around.

What are the advantages of having multiple sets of chromosomes?

Plants which show this phenomenon tend to have larger cells, because the nucleus is bigger than normal to accommodate the increased numbers of chromosomes. Leaves tend to be thicker and fleshier and the fruit larger; an altogether more desirable crop!

Wheat requires a temperate climate with a definite cold spell to encourage germination and early growth; more than 750 mm of rainfall per year and bright summers for harvesting. Variations on this climate cause problems; it will not grow well in tropical conditions, nor if the rainfall is too high. In the UK wheat is grown mainly in the south where the conditions are more in tune with its requirements. The main type of wheat grown in the UK is referred to as 'soft' wheat. It has a relatively low protein content and is used to make biscuits, confectionery and as animal feed.

Wild 'einkorn', the ancestral stock for modern wheat is a low-yielding species still found cultivated today in Turkey. It is believed to have cross bred with a grass growing as a weed in neighbouring fields. The resulting seeds developed into a tetraploid crop with a chromosome number of 28 – *Triticum durum* (Durum wheat). Readily grown in the Mediterranean and India, it is low in gluten levels and used for making pasta – the 'macaroni wheat'.

This wheat is of little value in bread making because it is low in gluten, the protein responsible for trapping carbon dioxide while the mixture is 'proving', allowing the dough to rise. As a result of natural mutation a hexaploid wheat strain has developed containing increased levels of gluten, producing an altogether spongier loaf of bread! Referred to as 'hard' wheat, *Triticum aestivum* contains 42 chromosomes (3 times that of einkorn) and grows best in North America and Russia where there is limited rainfall and long hot summers. It is a cross between *Triticum durum* and a local grass.

Biotechnology and wheat

With the advent of modern farming methods and an increase in our understanding of science the artificial evolution of wheat has accelerated. Demand for specific characteristics have dictated the properties of modern day wheat:

- *Shorter varieties*
  For decades genes for dwarfing have been bred into commercial wheats to increase the standing power of the crop. Shorter, stronger stems prevent the plants from being blown over in wet and windy weather.
- *Herbicide tolerance*
  Perhaps one of the earliest genetic modifications carried out on wheat was to selectively breed for a herbicide tolerant gene. This protects the crop from herbicides which would otherwise kill or damage it.
- *Improved gluten levels*
  The spongy, light texture of bread depends upon the elasticity of the dough, this in turn depends upon the elasticity of the protein – gluten. UK wheat is low in gluten levels and not suitable for bread making. It has to be fortified with flour imported from North America to improve its bread-making properties. Scientists have now identified genes associated with these properties and are working towards the transfer of these genes from good bread-making wheat into UK wheat or the modification of genes in UK wheat.

Frankenstein foods and blue bananas

The story of wheat began with human selection of natural varieties. Genetic engineering has escalated artificial evolution of a crop so that it is far removed from its ancestral type, with the possibility of introducing genes derived from other organisms. To this end, genetic engineering can be regarded as a more precise form of selective breeding. It allows scientists to make an accurate selection of the characteristics contained in an organisms genes and to transfer that information to another organism. By identifying the gene/s responsible for desirable characteristics, isolating these genes and transferring them via a carrier or vector to another species, it is possible to combine desirable characteristics from unrelated organisms. It has been made possible by four main developments over the last 30 years:

- Scientists discovered a group of enzymes which have the ability to cut DNA at specific locations so that individual genes can be removed from the chromosome.
- The discovery of another group of enzymes which are able to rejoin lengths of DNA together.
- The discovery that bacteria could be used to reproduce large quantities of identical pieces of DNA, a technique known as genetic cloning.
- The development of techniques which allowed the location of genes on particular chromosomes to be identified, known as gene mapping.

By using a combination of these techniques, it is possible to take a gene coding for a particular characteristic in one organism and transfer it to a different organism (see Figure 8.5). The advantages of such technology to agriculture have been varied and far reaching. It is now possible to grow strains of the same crop with different commercial end-uses in mind. The pea, for example, may be used as a food source for humans and animals, but it also has uses in the cosmetics industry for the manufacture of lipsticks. Within the last 5–10 years there has been considerable investment by the agro-industrial companies in research into the commercial use of genetically engineered microorganisms (GEMS). These organisms are being developed to:

- provide protection for crops from pests, disease and environmental stress, reducing the dependence on chemical fertilisers and pesticides;
- improve the ability of plants to obtain minerals from the soil;
- accelerate the breakdown of toxic waste materials by biological means, thereby removing pollutants already in the environment.

The field of 'plant' resistance to disease, or insect damage for example, has been an important target of research for many years. Oilseed rape is perhaps the most heavily studied and modified of all crops. Although genetically engineered varieties have only recently been introduced into the UK, selectively modified forms have been grown in this country for many years. Concar and Coghlan (1999) explain that one particular form of oilseed rape, known to Canadian

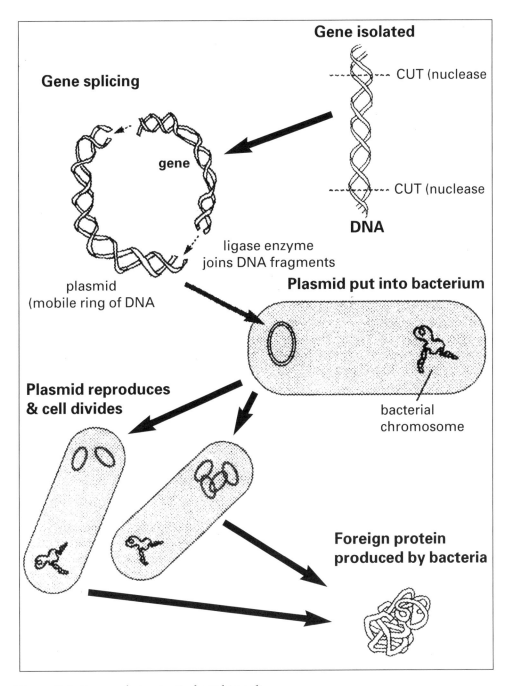

Figure 8.5 Gene splicing in *Escherichia coli*

farmers as 'Smart Canola' '. . . carries genes for resistance to two families of herbicides, the farmers can kill off every weed in sight, without fear of damaging their harvest' (1999, p. 4). They go on to explain that scientists used normal breeding and selection techniques to create Smart Canola. This necessitated screening thousands of naturally occurring strains that were resistant to herbicides, to select the most suitable. By its nature, this is a lengthy process because selection is based on the phenotype and this takes time to develop.

More recently, the use of gene technology has been employed within this area. It is now possible to make plants virus-resistant by introducing a gene from the relevant virus into the plant. This procedure has been so successful that virus-resistant tobacco is already grown commercially in China.

As well as improving the growth of crops and their resistance to pests, it is possible to alter them so that the end product for harvest has a better mix of the essential nutrients for a balanced diet. This involves the introduction of genes for the production of additional vitamins, amino acids and the storage of vital minerals.

In the horticultural industry, damage to crops incurred during transportation and deterioration during display costs farmers several millions of pounds. Biotechnology has the potential to reduce wastage by devising novel methods for the control of important processes in fruit and vegetable maturation, allowing them to stay fresher for longer.

Based on a better understanding of the ripening process of tomatoes, scientists have genetically engineered a variety which ripens but does not spoil during the process or during transportation and storage. When an unaltered tomato ripens, its texture is determined by a single gene. This gene produces an enzyme that slowly degrades the cell walls of the fruit, leading to the familiar mushy texture of over-ripe tomatoes. When the enzyme controlling this process is inhibited, the fruit ripens in the normal way, but does not over-ripen and spoil. Tomatoes produced in this way develop colour and aroma in an identical fashion to untreated tomatoes but with improved flavour because they are able to ripen on the plant for longer. These tomatoes can be found in cans on the shelves of two leading supermarkets here in Britain, (see Figure 8.6).

This technique has been developed to produce vegetable oil from oilseed rape; and even a genetically engineered decaffeinated coffee bean. On a more environmental scale, with climate change becoming a threat to ecosystems (see Chapter 5), the call for new varieties of key crops has been on the increase. To gain maximum yield, the flowering of crops such as wheat must be precisely tuned to environmental conditions, notably temperature and day length. Plant breeders and geneticists are identifying the genetic basis of improved varieties to provide UK farmers with an extended range of flowering and maturity times, giving improved climatic adaptability and better yields. This knowledge will help the maintenance of present UK yield levels if climates change as predicted. It also offers scope for improving adaptability and yields of varieties grown in developing countries where restricted seasons make precision timing of flowering particularly important.

Figure 8.6 Genetically engineered tomatoes

BST or mammoth cows!

Genetic manipulation has not been restricted to the plant kingdom. Perhaps the best known and highly controversial example of genetic engineering in livestock has been the production of the animal protein, bovine somatotropin (BST). BST is important because it is one of several hormones that animals produce which influence the efficiency with which food is converted into body protein or milk. Increased amounts of BST result in faster weight gain in animals used for meat production and higher milk yields in cows. The artificial production of BST has enabled large amounts to be produced economically for regular use in agriculture. Concerns about overproduction of milk and the threat to farm employment have meant that BST is not available for sale in Europe. In countries such as Russia, where milk and meat are in short supply, there is enormous demand for BST to help increase supplies.

From Polly to Dolly

The use of genetic engineering has equally been applied to medicine. This hit the headlines with the development of Polly, a transgenic sheep containing the human blood clotting gene for treatment of haemophilia. Then came the arrival of Dolly, a cloned sheep created from udder cells inserted into the egg cell of a surrogate ewe. The DNA from the egg had previously been removed, so the genetic material introduced from the udder cell was transcribed and translated during incubation. The end product was Dolly.

If this makes you feel weak at the knees, you could always reach for the latest in pick-me-up remedies: a colour coded banana containing the gene for paracetamol. It does not actually exist, but it could do!

Feeding the world

Genetic engineering has been heralded as a potential solution to the global food crisis. The development of crops tolerant to drought, frost or saline conditions would increase food production in marginal areas. There is however a real need to win over consumer confidence with regards to the GM debate. Non-genetic scares such as BSE and *E. Coli* have severely shaken this confidence and trust and resulted in the current controversy over the whole food production industry.

In 1993 the Polkinghorne Committee (1993) recognised public concern and suggested that food products containing genes of human origin and other 'ethically sensitive' copy genes should be labelled and if possible, suitable alternatives used. It was not however until March 1999 that legislation requiring the labelling of all foods containing genetically modified ingredients, was introduced.

The thinking behind this is that the consumer can then decide for themselves whether or not they wish to eat GM foods. Levitt (1999) questions the value of this, stating that if the '. . . issues are to do with long-term damage to the environment or to the economies of the Third World countries, should individual consumers be left to decide about these products for themselves?' (p. 106). Levitt goes on to explain that objection to GM usage in foods is fueled by the reality of the situation in the United States of America. He cites the recent announcement by Monsanto of its intention to build a $550 million factory producing the herbicide 'Roundup' in Brazil, which was shortly followed by the Brazilian Government approving 'Roundup' resistant soya beans as the countrys first GM crop. Levitt suggests that the soya will benefit the big landowners who will feed it to their cattle for export, but the majority of subsistence farmers will not benefit because they cannot afford to grow soya. He states that it is '. . . unrealistic to expect the biotechnology industry to bring about the necessary redistribution of wealth to enable small farmers in poorer countries to benefit from the research and sale of patented genes' (Levitt, p. 106).

The need to know . . .

If modern biotechnology is to be used as a means of overcoming the global food problem, more needs to be known about it. At the time of writing, concern focuses on possible risks to humans, to wildlife and the environment. Hertiage (1999, p. 100) urges us to consider these new advances on their merits '. . . weighing benefits against risks and coming to a rational conclusion, based on science and not on sentiment'. Many decisions will need to be made by today's children who are the decision-makers of tomorrow. They will be expected to play a full and responsible role in society, making decisions and taking action on the major issues of the day. These actions and decisions need to be informed.

When we refer back to the opening paragraph of this chapter, it appears that there is a fundamental need to educate children not just about the modern advances of genetics but about the fundamentals of food and food production. In response to the MORI poll carried out on behalf of the National Farmers' Union, the NFU now supports more than 120 farms around the UK in opening their gates to help educate children about farming and food products. This, at a time when the farming industry is in crisis, is a tremendous step forward, but 'food and food production' needs to be reinstated into the school curriculum. The new National Curriculum 2000 illustrates some recognition, with the study of food being compulsory for 11–14 year olds. Yet food habits begin earlier than that, with many primary children being just as vulnerable to poor diets as their secondary counterparts.

All too often children are living off fast foods which offer little nutritionally and do little to excite the taste buds. Much of the fruit and vegetables we receive in our shops have been 'forced' and the taste is often bland. Current research into a more flavoursome tomato is being carried out to return the flavours lost by years of high productivity. This is an absurd scenario whereby we have to rectify a situation artificially in order to regain a natural characteristic.

Harvey and Passmore (1995) suggest that if children are to take a greater interest in the food they eat, where it has come from and how it has been produced, then what is taught in schools must be more in tune with the issues of our everyday lives. This is reinforced by the National Curriculum Council's guidance document which aims to support schools in providing healthier food choices (NCC 1990a). The document promotes the 'whole school' approach to healthy eating and suggests that what is being taught about food and nutrition is reinforced by quality food and drink being provided in the canteen, thereby promoting the importance of a balanced and varied diet for all.

Summary

This chapter has traced agricultural practices since the development of the early human settlements; turning to the future, it has highlighted the potential global food crisis and explored possible means of overcoming it. The advantages and disadvantages of the various approaches have been discussed, at the same time recognising the need to raise public awareness of the associated issues. This served to highlight the fundamental flaws in our understanding of food and diet. If, as suggested our children's taste buds are being 'switched-off' by current culinary delights and we aim to switch them back on by artificially produced flavours, what does the future hold for them? Unless children are given a sound foundation on which to develop and appreciate a full range of flavours, we may find biotechnology being employed in producing 'Pizza' flavoured fish; chocolate flavoured meat and the enticing 'blue bananas'!

Chapter 9
Health and our bodies

Michael Littledyke

The notion of environment is not necessarily restricted to the external world. In this chapter, therefore, we focus on the idea of our bodies as an internal environment. The principles of environmental reason and environmental ethics, as discussed in Chapter 3, apply in this dimension as they do in the wider concept of environment. However, in this case, individuals have more potential for direct control over their health patterns through lifestyle choices than they do over wider environmental issues (though it should be acknowledged that this potential for control is limited under conditions of poverty). Choices of lifestyle can have direct impact on health, hence the importance of understanding about healthy functioning of the body and problems of ill-health. Scientific understanding of how our bodies work can inform these choices, while the application of ethics is primarily through care of ourselves. Taking care of our bodies by activities which promote health is the area where we may exert the most direct influence on the quality of our lives, hence it is a particularly important area for children to learn about.

The chapter covers a potentially wide field of knowledge which is, of necessity, presented in summarised form. This is useful background knowledge for the teacher which will need to be adapted to plan teaching programmes to suit particular ages and experience of children.

The chapter will address the following questions. Try answering them as a preliminary to reading, and reflect on how your own lifestyle choices may be influenced by your understanding of the health consequences of various kinds of action.

- *Health concepts*
  What does it mean to be healthy?
  What must we do to keep healthy?
  What are the implications for health education at Key Stages 1 and 2?
- *Materials and energy audit*
  What substances enter the body and how are they used?
  How do they eventually leave the body?

Which substances are healthy, which may be unhealthy and why?

What happens to energy transferred during respiration?

- *Body systems and functions*

  What are the common properties of living things and how are these achieved by our main body systems?

  Where are the main body organs and organ systems, and what are their main functions? How can they be kept healthy? What may damage them?

- *Action for health*

  What are healthy or unhealthy activities and what effects do they have on the various parts and functions of the body?

  How does this influence the choices we may make in our lives?

This is a topic where personal, social and health education clearly overlaps with science, and the opportunity to link them should not be missed. Traditional approaches to teaching about the body, which develop biological concepts without relating them to direct experience, can produce rote learning which has no significance to a person's life. This is a wasted opportunity to learn about something which is of vital importance to everyone. The primary purpose of learning about how our bodies work must surely be to inform our lifestyle choices which can impact directly upon health and the wider environment. This makes understanding of the biological concepts and the consequences of actions which influence health of great importance to the lives of individuals.

What does it mean to be healthy?

Views of health have changed over the years. For example, near the end of last century, when life expectancy was much lower (47 for men and 50 for women in 1870, compared to 75 for men, 80 for women in 1990), health was generally seen as the absence of disease. As living conditions and health expectations improved, views of health changed. A World Health Organisation statement in 1947 defined health as '. . . a state of complete physical, mental and social well being and not merely the absence of disease or infirmity' (cited in Pecujac 1998). This was a more positive definition of health which also goes beyond bodily health. It was limited, however, in that it implied that health was only possible for fully able bodied persons. It did not take into account, for example, that a blind person could be otherwise healthy. It also did not consider the social context of health. More recent views see health in a more inclusive and holistic context, for example:

> Good health implies the achievement of a dynamic balance between individuals (or groups) and their environment: To the individual, good health means improved quality of life, less sickness and disability, a happier personal, family and social existence, and the opportunities to make choices at work and recreation . . . To the community, good health means a higher standard of living, greater participation in making and implementing community health policies and reducing health care costs. (Better Health Commission 1986, cited in Pecujac 1998)

Health, then, is about our lives and condition as individuals, but also about social conditions and relationships and how that impacts on individuals.

There are four broad components of health; physical, social, emotional and spiritual. Figure 9.1 illustrates the dynamic interaction between these components and how each aspect can affect the others. This confirms that any consideration of the body and health should also take into account the wider influences. When teaching about the body and health it is, therefore, also important to consider what kinds of social relationships, attitudes and feelings about other people and the world will contribute to health.

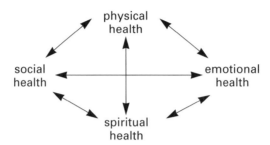

Figure 9.1 The dynamics of health

A summary of some of the key influences on the four components of health follows.

Physical health

Physical health is affected by factors such as fitness, muscle tone, efficient functioning of body organs, appropriate body weight, which can be influenced by lifestyle choices, such as physical activity, use of drugs or choice of food. Some factors such as stress or environmental pollution may be controlled to some degree by stress management techniques or by choice of place to live. However, this may be difficult to achieve for people of low educational background on lower incomes in deprived and difficult social conditions. Genetic make-up affecting body type, resistance to disease, or capacity to recover from illness are factors which may be beyond personal control, though lifestyle choices play an important part in how genetic predispositions are expressed. Physical health can be confirmed by physical observations and measurements, such as pulse rate, blood pressure, body size and fitness. It can also be a visible indicator of poor conditions for social, emotional or spiritual health.

Social health

We rely on and interact with many people, such as family, friends, shop assistants, work or school colleagues. The quality of interactions, ability to form relationships, interact with friends and the community, or enjoy social situations all affect health. Everyone has a need for love, esteem, a sense of place in society and feeling of belonging in a community (Maslow 1968). School can play a significant role in achieving this for children by modelling and valuing positive, caring and supportive relationships (Charlton and David 1989).

Across the population, the social and cultural context, such as nationality, education level, family background, whether employed or not, and levels of poverty, shape attitudes and behaviour, which affect health. In particular, poorer sections of society are often associated with higher rates of smoking and drinking, crowded living, poor diet, lower levels of education, lack of social support and low self esteem. This can directly reduce health. For example, Aborigines are among the poorest social groups in Australia and as a group exhibit the poorest health indicators. Their life expectancy is 55 for men and 60 for women, compared to 75 for men and 80 for women across the rest of the population. In the UK poorer groups also have lower life expectancies as well as higher incidence of major illnesses such as cancer and heart disease.

The political environment can also affect health. Hence, improvements in education and employment may improve health among economically deprived groups while laws may promote health by, for example, restricting access to harmful drugs (reducing damage to the body), enforcing seat belts (reducing accident injuries), or limiting CFC use or lead in petrol (reducing pollution). Decisions about allocation of funds to health care and initiatives to produce a better environment are other ways in which political decisions affect health.

Emotional health

Emotional health is influenced by self-esteem and confidence, hence an important aspect of health promoting in school is to develop confidence and emotional balance in children. This has a direct impact on learning, as confidence, self-esteem and motivation to learn are closely linked with achievement. A supportive environment where individuals are valued and where problems are aired is also important in helping individuals to cope with social problems and pressures to make unhealthy lifestyle choices as well as dealing with stress and anger. Mental health affects choices and action. This is illustrated by the increasing numbers of teenagers who suffer from depression, which is commonly associated with poor self-esteem, often leading to poor lifestyle choices such as drug taking or smoking.

Self image can affect health significantly. Ideal image has changed significantly throughout history and can vary by culture; for example, in the western world, women in medieval art have exaggeratedly rounded paunches, showing what was attractive then, while large breasts, flat abdomens and narrow hips were fashionable in the 1950s. Since the 1960s a generally slimmer body has been regarded as stylish, which puts pressure on women, men and children to keep unreasonably thin. Young girls are particularly susceptible, and this can lead to anorexia, bulimia and binge eating, with severe health implications. In contrast, by African or Jamaican standards, big equals beautiful and in these cultures there is less pressure to conform to unreasonable stereotypes.

The influences of body image in fashion advertising is worth discussing with children, as they are inevitably subject to these influences and need to be aware of the potential harmful effects to health if excessive dieting regimes are followed. Whilst recognising that obesity through overeating is also damaging to health, it is also important to recognise that humans have a range of body sizes due to genetic influences. Thus, large and small framed people can be equally healthy and attractive, though each person has direct influence on their own health, particularly through diet and activity.

Spiritual health

The basis of spiritual health may be religious, humanistic or environmental. Underpinning this is a caring outlook which also involves a sense of belonging and a feeling of being part of a wider world. As we care for others we also care for ourselves, and others may reciprocate in kind. This relationality and belonging is an important part of life which gives a sense of purpose and meaning. The consequent feeling of well being is an aspect of health. Members of some religious groups, for instance, have marginally longer life expectancy than other members of the population, while members of tribal groups, such as Native Americans, Aborigines and Innuits, who have had their traditional culture wrecked by western influences, may exhibit symptoms of depression, reduced health and shorter life expectancies.

Approaches to religious and environmental education will support this sense of belonging, as religion is concerned with spiritual ways of being and fostering a personal relationship with the divine, whilst ecology is intrinsically concerned with relationships of living things. Science offers rational support for this perspective, as biology confirms that we as humans are continuous with all life on this planet through a shared history, common ancestors (shown by evolution) and common characteristics (demonstrated by genetics and physiology). All living things have similar physiology at the cellular level, as all undergo cellular respiration, and all share DNA as genetic information which directs development (Chapter 7). Science shows us that all of life is truly one family. This perspective also demolishes such prejudiced and scientifically ignorant views as concepts of supposed racial superiority. A scientific analysis of human diversity confirms far more similarity than difference, as all humans are very much a part of a close genetic family. Of some 100,000 or so active genes, a mere handful are linked to skin colour. Also, the genetic variation within black Africa is far greater than all the rest of the variation in the human population. Supposed racial difference is in a very real sense only skin deep, as we humans are all very much more similar than we are different. It is this sense of connectedness which lies at the basis of a spiritual view of the world.

Health education

Health education is the means by which these issues are dealt with in the curriculum. This is one of the cross-curricular themes identified by the National Curriculum Council in 1989. By definition health education promotes:

> A quality of life and the physical, social and mental well-being of the individual. It covers the provision of information about what is good and what is harmful and involves the development of skills which help individuals to use their knowledge effectively. (NCC 1990b)

It is not an additional subject but should be addressed as a whole-school issue taught through the subjects of the National Curriculum. Curriculum science clearly has an important role to play in this respect. However, a whole-school issue is one that affects everyone: pupils, teaching staff, non-teaching staff, parents, governors and members of the community. A whole-school approach to health education ensures that guidelines are laid down, usually in a policy document. These guidelines should enable everyone to become actively involved in the process of providing an environment, ethos, curriculum and structures which positively support the fundamental health and safety principle. This principle should:

- value young people;
- care about young people;
- provide opportunities for developing positive self images.

These foundations give pupils the opportunity to learn the skills they need to be safe and healthy in any situation.

Health education policy

Within the aims of any good school we expect to find statements about the development of the self-esteem of pupils and relationships both within the school and with the wider community. An example of such policy statements follows:
A health promoting school aims:

- to actively promote the self-esteem of all pupils by demonstrating that everyone can make a contribution to the life of the school;
- to develop good staff/pupil and pupil/pupil relationships in the daily life of the school;
- to make clear to staff and pupils, the social aims of the school to provide stimulating challenges for all pupils through a wide range of activities;
- to take every opportunity to enhance the physical environment of the school;
- to develop good school/home/community links and share activities;
- to develop good links between associated primary/secondary schools in planning a coherent health education curriculum;
- to promote staff health and well-being;
- to consider the exemplar role of staff in health-related issues;

- to consider the complementary role of school policies to the health education curriculum, e.g. policies on smoking, bullying, healthy eating;
- to use the potential of specialist services in the community for advice and support in health education;
- to develop the education potential of the school health services beyond routine screening and towards active support for the curriculum.

(modified from The Scottish Health Education Group and World Health Organisation 1989)

The NCC publication *Curriculum Guidance: 5 Health Education* (1990b) lists the following elements of health education:

Substance use and misuse
Sex education
Family life education
Safety
Health related exercise
Food and nutrition
Personal hygiene
Environmental aspects of health education
Psychological aspects of health education

These elements can be readily addressed directly alongside a science topic on the body, as they all have direct impact on bodily health. The elements are incorporated into the following approach to finding out about the body and health.

Finding out about the body and health

The relevant part of the national curriculum concerns 'humans as organisms'. Health is indicated in the references to dental care, diet and tobacco, alcohol and other drugs (DfE 1995, Sc. 2, 2, pp. 40, 45). There are, however, implications about health throughout this topic which need to be made explicit, so that the concepts directly inform health issues. An approach to a topic on the body will therefore emphasise understanding of the various body organs, how and why they function as they do, how they contribute to keeping us healthy, what we can do to help them work well and what activities may harm them. The wider issues concerning health education, the social, emotional and spiritual factors, can be developed at the same time.

A useful elicitation starter concerning what is in the body is to ask the children to draw on body outlines what they think is inside the body (as provided by the Nuffield Primary Science Scheme 1995, for example). This provides useful information to the teacher about children's initial understanding and starting points. A follow-up activity, after discussion about the location of the main organs could be to draw a large outline of a child, paste cut outs of the main organs and indicate what the main functions are. The significance of the vital organs, the heart, lungs and brain, should be emphasised, as loss of function of these causes death, hence the importance of good maintenance. Use of a model torso showing the position of internal organs, reference books or CD ROMs is important to help fill in the details.

A useful way of identifying the functions of the various body systems is through the properties of living things (DfE 1995, Sc. 2, 1a and b, pp. 40, 45). This approach shows that all living things have certain properties in common and all forms of animals and plants have particular body structures and functions to help them carry these out. The seven properties are movement, respiration, sensitivity, growth, reproduction, excretion and nutrition (a useful mnemonic is MRS GREN). The main biological aim is to reproduce, whilst the other six properties are concerned with gaining materials and energy to survive and achieve the passing on of genes to the next generation. Table 9.1, which was developed as plans for part of a Year 5 teaching programme, shows a summary of the main ideas linking the properties of living things, why they are necessary for survival, how humans carry them out and what is healthy or unhealthy. More details were included in the actual teaching. However, making links in this way helps to establish the 'big ideas' and show what are the essential functions, which helps to make clear what life choices may maintain health or otherwise.

A materials audit: What materials go in, what happens to them in the body and how and in what form do they come out again?

Another useful way to establish some of the 'big ideas' about the body and health is to find out what enters and leaves the body from a matter and energy point of view; what goes in, what happens to it in the body and how and in what form it comes out. This will help to make clear what may be healthy and unhealthy materials to take into the body. A useful analogy to make is that the body is like a finely tuned machine which needs the best materials put into it (healthy food, water, clean air), as well as good servicing and maintenance (suitable activity; exercise and rest) to make it work well, and good waste disposal (from the lungs, skin, kidneys and gut).

Figure 9.2 illustrates the main points. The body uses 90 per cent of its food intake as fuel (the other 10 per cent is used to provide materials for growth and repair). Fuel food and oxygen, are taken in and transported by the digestive, respiratory and circulatory systems respectively to the cells all over the body, where respiration takes place and energy is released for use in movement (through muscle action), growth and repair of tissues and body heat production. Digested fuel food is transported in the blood as glucose, and blood sugar level is under the control of insulin secreted by the pancreas. Food used as material for growth, mainly digested proteins (amino acids), is also available from blood to provide materials for dividing cells. Undigested food is egested as faeces through the anus. Excess fuel food is stored in the liver (as glycogen) or as fat until it is needed. Regular overeating may lead to obesity.

What are all living things able to do? They can all:	Why do animals need to do this?	Which parts of our body do this?	What can we do to keep these parts healthy?	What will make these parts unhealthy?
move	to find the best conditions to live, find food, avoid danger, find a mate, look after young	skeleton and muscles	exercise eat food which makes strong bones (e.g. calcium in milk/dairy products)	no exercise poor diet
use air (oxygen) and fuel for energy (respire)	to get energy to live and do all the other things in the list	all body cells (lungs take in oxygen, gut takes in fuel)	exercise breathe clean air	no exercise smoking affects oxygen intake
be sensitive to their surroundings	to do all the things listed under movement	brain, eyes, ears, tongue, nose, skin	good food (e.g. vitamin A in carrots helps eyesight) be alert/active	being lazy poor food
grow (based on cell division)	to grow to an adult and have young	all over	balanced diet of carbohydrates, fat, protein, vitamins and minerals	unbalanced diet
have young (reproduce)	so they continue to live in their young/don't die out	genitals/reproductive organs	keep clean – hygiene good food	not washing poor food
get rid of wastes (includes urea and CO_2) (excrete)	they would otherwise be poisoned and die	kidneys, bladder	drink plenty	not enough liquid excess alcohol
get food (nutrition)	to grow replace worn out cells provide a fuel supply of respiration	digestive system (blood transports food, O_2 for respiration, removes wastes)	balanced diet – not too much (obesity) or too little (anorexia)	unbalanced diet

Table 9.1 The body and health

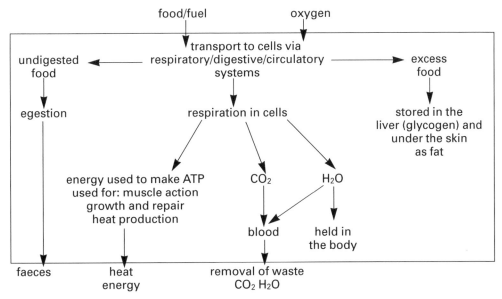

Figure 9.2 The movement of materials through the body

A simplified summary of the process of respiration is (with the summarised chemical formula, relevant to key stage 3, below):

$$\text{fuel} \quad + \quad \text{oxygen} \quad = \quad \text{carbon dioxide} \quad + \quad \text{water}$$

$$C_6H_{12}O_6 \qquad 6O_2 \qquad\qquad 6CO_2 \qquad\qquad 6H_2O$$
$$\text{(glucose)}$$

This reaction is a summary of a series of reactions which drive the ADP (adenosine diphosphate) to ATP (adenosine triphosphate) reaction. Energy is transferred by converting 6 ADP molecules and 6 phosphate groups to 6 ATP molecules.

The energy released through respiration in the cells is taken up and stored by making a stable molecule of ADP into a highly reactive, weakly bonded molecule of ATP. The energy is released when it is needed when the third weak phosphate bond is replaced by a strong bond. Heat energy is transferred as waste, which helps to keep the body temperature at the correct level for cell activities, and is eventually lost to the surroundings of the body. Carbon dioxide and water are produced as material waste and pass into the blood. Water is needed in the cells, but excess water is excreted through the skin, kidneys and lungs. Carbon dioxide is transported to the lungs where it is excreted through exhalation.

Having determined the significance of the body systems, how the energy requirements of the body are met, where the main organs are located and their main functions, it is now relevant to look at each system. However, it should be emphasised that the systems interact closely to provide the conditions for healthy life even though it is necessary to look at the systems separately to make sense of what each does. It is not possible to include all details here, but the key points will be identified.

Digestive system and liver

The digestive system breaks up food physically (mastication in the mouth) and chemically (digestion by enzymes in the digestive tract) so that it can pass into our blood and be transported around the body to enter our cells. The food is needed as a fuel (90 per cent as fats and carbohydrates) to provide energy (combines with oxygen) and to provide materials for growth and repair (10 per cent mostly as proteins).

Table 9.2 shows the functions of the components of the digestive system.

A balanced diet is particularly important for health. This must include appropriate amounts of the following:

- *Carbohydrates* are fuel foods found as starch (e.g. bread, potatoes, pasta, cereals and sugar). Digestion of carbohydrate breaks it into sugar (glucose) which enters the blood, though concentrated sugar as food (in table sugar, sweets, chocolate which contains sucrose) is unhealthy if eaten in large amounts. Cellulose (fibre or roughage found in plant foods) is an indigestible, but important carbohydrate which keeps the food moving through

Part	Function
Buccal cavity/salivary glands (mouth)	Ingestion, mastication (mechanical digestion), starch digestion (chemical digestion through salivary enzyme)
Pharynx (throat)	Swallowing
Oesophagus (food tube)	Links pharynx to stomach, peristalsis
Stomach (not to be confused with 'tummy' or 'belly')	Churns food, protein digestion through enzymes in gastric juice, hydrochloric acid kills bacteria
Duodenum	Digestion, absorption of food into blood
Gall bladder	Bile (produced by liver) emulsifies fats
Pancreas	Enzymes secreted which digest carbohydrates, protein, fats Insulin secretion (for control of blood sugar level)
Ileum (small intestine)	Enzymes secreted Increased surface area for digestion and absorption of food into blood through folds and finger-like projections (villi)
Caecum and appendix	Vestigial (evolutionary remnant) – no function (bacteria digest cellulose in herbivores, e.g. cow)
Colon (large intestine)	Absorption of water
Rectum (large intestine)	Formation and storage of faeces Bacteria digest some food and add vitamins
Anus	Egestion/defecation of undigested (unused) food
Liver	Receives all digested food and makes it suitable to be used by the body

Table 9.2 The digestive system and liver

the gut (note that some animals such as cows and termites can digest cellulose, because of specialised bacteria in their guts).

- *Proteins* are structural materials used for growth and repair. They are present in most foods but are particularly abundant in animal foods (e.g. milk, eggs, meat) and some plants (e.g. beans, lentils, nuts). Digestion breaks them into amino acids which enter the blood, where cells which are growing can use them to rebuild proteins.
- *Fats* are a concentrated fuel, transferring large amounts of energy when respired, and act as an energy reserve in the body. Fats contain fatty acids which can be saturated (cannot possess more hydrogen atoms – mainly animal fats) or unsaturated (have room for more atoms – mainly plant fats). Excessive eating of saturated fats is linked with heart disease.
- *Minerals* are important for a range of functions, such as blood composition (sodium), haemoglobin in red blood cells (iron), bones and teeth (calcium, phosphorous) etc.
- *Vitamins* also have a range of functions and are needed for health, e.g. vitamin A is important for eyes, aiding sight in dim light, B vitamins are used for many different chemical processes in the body, vitamin C helps cells stick together (hence bleeding gums in scurvy) and contributes to defence against disease, vitamin D is needed for bone development, vitamin E is needed for development of ovaries and testes, vitamin K aids blood clotting. Most vitamins are small, but complex molecules which our cells are unable to synthesise, but are essential for healthy living.
- *Water* is essential for life and all cell activities can only take place in solution (our bodies are about 70 per cent water).

Having too much of a food can be as harmful as too little, as Table 9.3 shows. However, eating well can actively help prevent disease as well as avoid it. For example, fruit and vegetables containing antioxidants and vitamins A, C, E, and some minerals can offer some cancer protection. Fibre also protects against bowel cancer.

In general, the problems of deficiency (but not lack of fibre) are often problems of third world poverty, whilst problems of excess (and lack of fibre) are often linked to affluent countries, though poorer sections of society may also exhibit deficiency symptoms.

Children need to understand which foods are good sources of the different categories for a balanced diet. A traffic light display of foods is a useful way of identifying healthy and potentially unhealthy food. The colours represent healthy (green – go ahead, e.g. fruit and vegetables), foods which should be eaten in controlled amounts (amber – go carefully, e.g. eggs and cheese), and foods which should be closely regulated (red – stop and think e.g. chips, chocolate, sweets). It is also useful to keep records of daily food intake and compare with charts or log into customised computer programmes which calculate the proportion of carbohydrates, proteins, fats to see if the diet is balanced.

Problems of excess	Problems of deficiency
Excess sugar – is linked to dental decay, diabetes and obesity *Excess salt* – is linked with stomach cancer, high blood pressure and heart disease *Excess fat* – is linked with heart disease (through constriction of artery diameter from cholesterol deposits), cancer, obesity, gall bladder disease, diabetes Some *artificial food additives* and *environmental pollutants* are associated with a range of illnesses, including asthma, cancers, heart disease	*Lack of fibre* – is linked to bowel disease, diverticulosis (pouching of the gut), constipation and bowel cancer *Marasmus* (general shortage of food) *Lack of* protein causes kwashiorkor *Lack of* calcium and vitamin D causes rickets *Lack of* iron causes anaemia *Lack of* iodine causes goitre *Lack of* vitamin A causes night blindness *Lack of* B vitamins causes pellegra and beri-beri *Lack of* vitamin C causes scurvy *Lack of* vitamin E causes sterility

Table 9.3 Dietary problems

Many primary schools ensure that food and drinks on offer in school canteens and tuck shops are restricted to those that contribute to healthy eating. Pupils need to be encouraged to make healthy choices within their diet and understand how to handle food safely.

This is also an excellent topic for investigating cultural variety through science. For example, investigate different diets from around the world, including their nutritional value and position in the food chain.

The liver

This is the largest organ (apart from the skin) and has many functions. It is the first place the blood visits with its new load of materials absorbed from the intestine. Here the liver has to remove or make safe any toxic substances, and correct the balance of various nutrients (see Table 9.2). Excess alcohol has the effect of damaging the liver and this can result in cirrhosis which involves hardening of the tissues, affecting their function. Some of the other functions of the liver include: storage of sugar as glycogen; vitamin and mineral storage; breakdown of excess amino acids (which make up protein); red blood cell breakdown; production of growth hormone and breakdown of excess other kinds of hormones; temporary blood storage; bile production for digestion of fats; heat production.

The breathing (ventilation) and respiratory system

Many children (and adults) think the air that comes in and out of the lungs is the same and do not realise that the waste material coming out of the lungs originates in the food we eat. The path of food we use for energy is as follows: from mouth to intestine, into blood, transport to cells, joins with oxygen, carbon dioxide is produced, back into blood, to lungs, out to air. The function of breathing (also called ventilation) is thus to get air into our bodies, and waste gases out. Respiration, on the other hand, is the process of combining food and oxygen to provide energy and takes place in the cells of the body.

Breathing (ventilation)

This process takes in air (providing us with oxygen) and removes carbon dioxide from the lungs. Water is also lost via this route as water vapour, as witnessed by 'seeing' your breath on a cold day. We make the lungs expand and contract by the diaphragm's muscular contraction (lowers diaphragm) and relaxation (diaphragm moves back into a dome shape) and by raising and lowering of the rib cage to increase and decrease the chest cavity. Differences in pressure between the air in the lungs and the air outside allow air to move one way or the other.

The lungs are like a sponge, a collection of thousands of tiny air sacs (alveoli) which are connected to the outside by tubes (numerous bronchioles arranged like a tree, larger bronchi and a cartilage-strengthened windpipe or trachea). The air sacs are surrounded by blood capillaries; oxygen levels are high in the air sacs and low in the blood so oxygen moves into the blood by diffusion, whilst carbon dioxide levels are high in the blood and low in the air sacs so carbon dioxide moves in to the air space. This transfer of gases is called gas exchange.

Respiration

This is where oxygen (carried by blood from the lungs) and digested food (carried by blood from the intestines) combine in the cells to transfer energy producing carbon dioxide and water (carried by blood to be excreted).

A very small amount of energy can be released if carbohydrate molecules are rearranged in the absence of oxygen (anaerobic respiration). The process can be useful if we need to get energy very quickly for a short burst, but the process builds up poisonous lactic acid in the muscle cells, which results in tiring and, if severe, causes cramp. Panting allows plenty of oxygen into the blood and the lactic acid combines with oxygen and can be metabolised fully.

There are a number of factors which can affect breathing/respiratory system, including asthma, smoking and exercise.

Asthma

Asthma is a disease affecting the airways, manifesting as short breath, coughing or wheezing. Causes may include allergies, pollution, strenuous exercise and nervous tension. Asthma decreases the capacity for breathing as the bronchi constrict. Treatments may include medication to dilate the bronchi to normal size. Asthma sufferers (especially children) are increasing in numbers, and this is thought to be linked to environmental factors, especially increasing pollution, particularly from traffic emissions.

Smoking

This is one of the most harmful activities for the body. Smoking causes an immediate decrease in the functioning of the lungs and the resistance to flow of air can increase by up to three times. Tobacco smoke inhalation (either directly or indirectly through 'passive' smoking) is damaging because of:

- tar, which is carcinogenic (causes cancer), forms a sticky coating on lungs when cool, and paralyses hairs in the nasal cavity which sweep invading bacteria out of the body;
- nicotine, which is highly addictive, damages brain structure and is poisonous (the nicotine in 10 packs of cigarettes will kill if injected directly – solution from cigarette ends in water also makes an effective insecticide against insects such as greenfly);
- carbon monoxide, which replaces oxygen in the blood, making the heart pump faster, leading to heart strain and possible heart attack. Carbon monoxide also helps the build up of cholesterol on blood vessel walls, affects eyesight (smokers see less well at night than non-smokers) and may cause reduced sensitivity to sounds.

Smoking can lead to chronic lung diseases, such as emphysema, bronchitis, smokers' cough, with damage to respiratory tubes, or cancer. The various effects of smoking are a major cause of death, with up to two out of five hospital beds being filled with patients suffering from smoking related disease.

Many schools acknowledge the hazards of passive smoking by becoming smoke-free environments. Not only does this protect the school community, but also sets a precedent for future work situations which may be encountered.

Exercise

Exercise has important beneficial effects on lung functioning. Heavy breathing from exercise keeps the airways free and improves the lungs' vital capacity (the amount of air moving in and out of the lungs), which directly affects oxygen uptake. Age will inevitably reduce the functioning of lungs, but exercise can keep the alveoli inflated and slow down the effects of ageing

Circulatory system

Many children think the blood is everywhere in the body. This is similar to the general view of a few centuries ago when people thought blood flowed away from the heart to nourish the body. William Harvey showed, however (in 1628), that blood circulates through a network of blood vessels with the heart as the pump. The body has double circulation with the heart pumping blood to the lungs picking up oxygen, and then to the body where food is respired with the oxygen and carbon dioxide is collected. The oxygenated and de-oxygenated blood are thus kept separate. This is necessary for active animals which regulate body temperature. In contrast, fish have single circulation with mixed blood and two heart chambers, whilst amphibians have partial separation of oxygenated and de-oxygenated blood in three heart chambers.

The blood transports materials around the body to supply the cells with food materials and oxygen. It also removes wastes. Hormones give chemical information for control of various parts of the body. The system also transports heat to keep limbs warm, or carries excess heat to the surface so we can keep cool. Blood contains about 55 per cent liquid (plasma) and 45 per cent solids made up of red cells (for transport of oxygen and carbon dioxide, though the latter is also carried in plasma), white cells (for defence against disease) and platelets (used in clotting).

Table 9.4 shows the elements of the circulatory system.

Poor diet and smoking affect the circulatory system, as described previously. In particular, fatty foods, excess salt and smoking all contribute to high blood pressure and heart disease. Restricted blood vessel diameter from build up of fatty deposits produces high blood pressure and there is a greatly increased chance of blood flow interruption, such as through a blood clot which blocks the passage (thrombosis). If this takes place in the coronary artery, which supplies the heart (coronary thrombosis), it can result in a heart attack, often with fatal effects, whilst interruption of blood flow to the brain will cause a stroke, which can result in paralysis or death.

Part	Function
Blood	Picks up and transports: • oxygen from lungs to tissues (as oxy-haemoglobin in red corpuscles) • digested food from digestive system to the cells • wastes from metabolism (e.g. urea from cells to the kidneys) • CO_2 (in plasma and red corpuscles) from cells to lungs • also transports blood clotting agents (platelets), hormones (from endocrine system), white cells (produce antibodies or ingest bacteria) and heat
Heart *Blood vessels* Arteries/arterioles Capillaries Venules/veins	Pumps blood around the body Carry blood around body Take blood from the heart (thick walled to withstand pressure) Exchange of materials with tissues, lymph formation Take blood to the heart (thin walled, with valves to prevent backflow)
Lymph vessels	Drain tissue spaces of excess fluid, lymph to blood circulation, fat transport
Lymph glands	Produce white cells which ingest foreign bodies or produce antibodies
Spleen/bone marrow	Produce red blood cells, spleen also acts as blood reservoir

Table 9.4 The elements of the circulatory system

Exercise has very beneficial effects on the circulatory system, resulting in more small blood vessels, more fuel and oxygen to working muscles, capacity for exercise at high intensity for longer, slower heart resting rate, more blood pumped to the heart and lower blood pressure.

Excretory system

The excretory system gets rid of the waste products of metabolism of the cells. The liver makes urea, which makes up urine, from waste nitrogenous products (note that carnivores have larger livers than herbivores since they use protein, which contains unwanted nitrogen, for fuel). This is passed into the blood and excreted via the kidneys which filter out the waste materials. The urine then travels to the bladder where it is stored before it is eliminated. This excreted material is sometimes confused with the egested material from the anus, the faeces, which has never really entered the body – it has remained undigested and unused in the digestive tract.

Other excretory organs are the lungs which eliminate carbon dioxide, and the skin which passes out certain salts and some urea.

Table 9.5 shows the elements of the excretory system.

Health factors and the lungs have been discussed previously. Health care of the other excretory organs, including the urinary system and the skin, are largely concerned with hygiene. Urinary infections may be caused by infrequent washing of the genital area or infrequent changing of underclothes. Such infections can also be transmitted during sex. Hygiene is also important in care of the skin, though a healthy diet with plenty of fresh foods and not too much fat is also important. We have natural skin bacteria which are important in healthy skin, so we should also be careful about not being over-hygienic through excessive uses of disinfectants, which can also cause pollution to rivers. Skin

Part	Function
Lungs	Water and carbon dioxide removed from blood
Kidneys	Ultrafiltration – small molecules removed from blood, e.g. water, glucose, urea
	Selective reabsorption – useful molecules reabsorbed, e.g. glucose
	Water control is through ADH (anti-diuretic hormone from pituitary gland in brain) – water intake stimulates less ADH i.e. water excreted, dehydration stimulates more ADH i.e. water retained
Linked to the kidneys are:	
Ureters	Tubes to the bladder
Bladder	Urine storage/emission
Urethra	Urine discharged
Skin (sweat glands)	Water and minerals released – usually associated with keeping cool

Table 9.5 The excretory system

cancer resulting from excessive exposure to sun is an increasing problem. This is particularly bad in Australia due to decreased ozone levels which normally act as a protection form damaging ultra violet rays. The prevalence of skin cancer has resulted in the 'slip slop slap' campaign to alert people to the problem (slip on a shirt, slop on a hat and slap on some suncream) (see Chapter 5 on ozone).

The muscle-skeleton system

Young children often have no awareness of the diversity of structure of bones and may draw them as double ended 'dog food' bones, even in the head. Getting children to feel the shape of different bones, and realise that they have different shapes and is an important experience for them.

The functions of the skeleton are:

- protection of vital organs (e.g. heart, lungs by the rib cage, brain by the skull, spinal cord by the vertebrae);
- movement (bones act as levers which are moved by muscles);
- support and body shape (bones act as a framework for the soft tissues);
- manufacture of blood cells (in certain bones e.g. vertebrae, sternum, parts of the skull and some long bones);
- mineral storage (99% of calcium is stored in bones, also phosphates, sodium and other minerals – this gives bone its hardness).

There are 206 different bones and over 200 joints in the body. The skeleton is made up of an *axial skeleton* (the central axis of the body – the skull, vertebral column, sternum and ribs) and the *appendicular skeleton* which is attached to it (including the appendages (arms and legs), shoulder (clavicle, scapula), pelvic girdle.

The types of bones are:

- long bones are used in movement: e.g. upper arm, thigh bone (humerus, femur);
- flat bones protect: e.g. skull, ribs, chest bone (sternum);
- short bones are used in less extensive movement: e.g. wrist (carpals), ankles (tarsals), fingers, toes (phalanges), kneecap (patella);
- irregular bones have specialised functions: e.g. spine (vertebrae), hip bone (pelvis), bones of the middle ear (malleus, incus, or hammer, anvil, stirrup).

Bone is made of *compact bone*, which is hard, on the outside, with *spongy bone* underneath, which is softer and with blood vessels. Red marrow found at the ends of long bones make red cells. Yellow marrow in the centre is made of fat cells and blood vessels. Bone is therefore alive: if a bone fractures it will re-grow. Protein fibres give it a degree of elasticity and tensile strength, whilst ossification, involving calcium phosphate deposits, give it hardness and compression strength.

Joints may be immovable (e.g. the fused bones of the skull), slightly moveable (separated by cartilage – e.g. vertebrae, the two bones of the pelvis) or freely moveable. Moveable bones are held together at their joints by ligaments which are made of material similar to tendons. To make joints operate smoothly, the ends of the bones are made of flexible cartilage, and a fluid (synovial fluid) which protects and lubricate. There are different types of moveable joints which allow different degrees of movement:

- gliding joints (e.g. carpals of the wrist which can slide over each other);
- hinge joints (e.g. arm-hinge joint which allows 180 degree movement);
- ball and socket joints (e.g. shoulder and hip joints allow 360 degrees movement);
- pivot joints (e.g. atlas and axis vertebrae of the neck allow some rotational movement of the head);
- twisting joints (allow twisting movement in two planes, e.g. metacarpals of the wrist and the thumb).

Movement needs muscles which are attached to the bones by the tendons, which are flexible but non-stretchy material. Muscles are attached to bones by tendons in antagonistic pairs which contract to move the bones in opposite directions (e.g. the biceps muscle flexes the arm and the triceps extends it).

Exercise is particularly important for healthy muscles. Regular exercise results in greater strength, ability to sustain position without fatigue and better recovery from injuries. Improved muscle tone from exercise also adds to the stability of joints, because stronger muscles hold the joints intact and assist in protecting them from damage. Additional benefits from exercise are improved circulatory and breathing/respiration functions, as well as increased concentration, less stress and less depression.

In contrast, lack of exercise results in decreased health through lower cardiovascular fitness, risk of higher blood pressure, diabetes, osteoporosis, cancer, anxiety and depression. Posture is affected by lifestyle; too much sitting results in increased lower back, neck and shoulder pain.

Pupils should understand the relationship between exercise and a healthy body. By offering a range of extra-curricular sporting and recreational activities suitable for all pupils, regardless of ability, the school can provide pupils with the opportunity for healthy exercise.

The nervous system

Why is it that animals have well developed senses, but plants have so few? Plants produce their own food through photosynthesis and are surrounded by what they need: light, air, water and minerals in the soil. They only need to grow the part of the plant towards the appropriate stimuli; leaves to light, roots to water, or to open and close the holes (stomata) on their leaves, or their flowers as conditions demand. When they need to move during sexual reproduction and dispersal of their seeds they use other agents such as animals or the wind to help them.

Animals, in contrast, generally need to move around to find the things they need for survival. They are unable to manufacture food and need to find food to eat; they need to find a mate; be able to disperse; and colonise new territory.

Complex animals, such as humans, have therefore developed specialised organs to detect light (eyes) sounds (ears) smells (nose) taste (tongue) and the sensation of touch (pressure, hot/cold).

The nervous system, including the brain, spinal chord (central nervous system), nerves (peripheral nervous system) and the sense organs, coordinates our responses to the world. Our brain is able to build up a picture of the world around us and it is through our senses that we perceive the world; all descriptions are linked with the sense organs. The sense organs work through nerves which are made up of nerve cells. Nerve cells communicate by sending electrical signals which may or may not pass from cell to cell through connecting gaps called synapses.

Muscles are stimulated to contract by nervous impulses. The route of nervous message to cause a muscle to contract is: sense organ (receptor), nerves to spinal chord (relay), to brain (interprets and sends instructions), back along spinal chord and nerves (relay), to muscles (effector-contracts). The electrical impulses travel through an ionic solution. The impulse is the same in all nerves and always travels at the same speed. The brain interprets differences in stimulus strength by the number of impulses, whilst the quality of the experience is related to which sense organs, which parts of the brain, or which muscles are involved. Nerve cells require to be re-set after each impulse has passed, and this requires energy, from respiration. Our brain consumes a large proportion of the food we use as fuel (some 50 per cent), and if it is starved of oxygen needed to respire the fuel for just a few minutes the nerve cells will die. This can result in various degrees of paralysis, or inhibited brain activity, or death.

A positive mental outlook is important for emotional and mental health. Developing positive outlooks through self-esteem, confidence and acceptance of self and others is a primary role of teachers, as this affects all aspects of learning. Pupils need to recognise that individuals may belong to many groups in which they have different roles. Within these groups individuals respond to events in different ways and these actions often have consequences for members of the group, therefore it is important to recognise and respect other people's emotions and feelings. Through these experiences pupils can understand the meaning of friendship and loyalty and begin to develop skills needed to form relationships.

Stressful environments can affect health and hinder learning. Stress is biologically useful through secretion of adrenaline from the adrenal glands (near the kidneys) into the bloodstream which prepares an animal for action, 'fight or flight'. A degree of stress is valuable in that it can motivate to appropriate action, be it on the sports field, or in preparation for mental activity. However, excessive stress through, for example, undue anxiety or aggressive, uncaring environments, may cause ill health manifest in tiredness, poor resistance to infections, or in chronic ailments such as ulcers. Counselling is a way of helping people to become aware of the problems in their lives and how they may manage these. An open atmosphere where problems are shared and discussed will help children in these matters and help foster good relationships in the group. These are crucial factors in the development of moral awareness and moral action in children. Drama strategies are particularly effective to achieve this (see Littledyke 1998 for a wide range of drama strategies for moral education).

Appropriate activity is also important for mental health. The body needs enough sleep. Sleep deprivation can result in general ill health and impaired learning. Exercise is also beneficial to mental health and is a major tool used by some to manage stress or depression. Endorphins are chemicals produced by the brain during and after exercise (and other activities such as laughter, sex and eating chocolate!) and are associated with feelings of well-being and positive states.

Intake of drugs, including alcohol, glue vapours, cannabis and the so called hard drugs, heroin, amphetamines and cocaine have direct action on the brain, affecting mental states, often with pleasurable feelings, but with possible long-term damage to health. There is increasing need for effective drugs education, including the effects on the body, as children are exposed more and more to these influences. Pupils should understand that all medicines are drugs, but not all drugs are medicines and that there are over-the-counter, prescribed and legal substances that play an important and beneficial role in society. Pupils should also know how to make choices and exercise some basic techniques for resisting pressure from friends and others to take potentially harmful drugs. Role play exercises and drama can be useful in exploring these issues.

Growth and reproductive systems

Living things are characterised by their ability to make more of themselves. Single celled bacteria do this by dividing into two. When we grow from the fertilised egg in our mother's womb that is also what happens. One cell divides into two, which divide into four, and so on. During growth cells also begin to specialise, and tissues such as muscle cells and nerve cells are formed to make up the organs and organ systems of the body. Once we are fully developed we still continue to grow and dead cells from all over the body are constantly replaced; for example, old skin drops off and contributes to house dust (and is food for the house mites) as new skin replaces the old; and half the cells in our liver are replaced every few months. Material for growth is provided by digested food in the blood; mostly amino acids that can be built up into new proteins. All of this is controlled by the genes in the nuclei of each cell.

Single celled organisms, such as bacteria or yeast, make clones (identical genetically) in order to reproduce. Sexual reproduction is most advantageous, however, because it creates variation by mixing of genes from two parents, and ultimately provides a range of characteristics in a population which can lead to evolution. (However, some variation in asexual reproduction is possible through mutations, allowing for evolution such as in the development of bacterial resistance to antibiotics.)

To guarantee that animals do reproduce themselves, ensuring survival of the species, evolution has ensured that males and females meet through elaborate attraction and mating behaviour which culminates in the pleasurable sensations of sex. Strong motivation for parental care also ensures in many species that offspring are looked after and protected after they are born. All these factors are relevant to we humans who are also motivated towards sex for the same reasons as other animals, though human sexuality can be complex because of social and cultural factors. Sex can play an important and fulfilling role in people's lives, but it can also be expressed exploitively and harmfully.

The processes of reproduction in outline follow. A sperm meets an egg, and the fertilised egg cell, now called a zygote, embeds itself in the uterus wall. After many cell divisions, accompanied by selective genes being switched on and off causing specialisation, the developing embryo becomes a foetus, then a baby. After nine months it is born by dilation of the neck of the uterus (cervix) and contraction of the uterine wall. The processes associated with sex and foetal development are controlled by a number of hormones, from the pituitary gland (in the brain) and from the ovaries (female hormones) and testes (male hormones).The developing embryo lives in a protective sack of water (the amnion) and gets its food and oxygen through the placenta, where the baby's blood and the mother's blood exchange materials (but not blood). At this stage, although the baby's heart beats to circulate food and oxygen received from the mother, the circulation from the baby's heart to its inactive lungs does not function. At birth the baby needs to empty its lungs of water and activate the heart fully, so its blood can start to visit the now functioning lungs.

Healthy diet (vitamin E, for example in water cress, wheat germ, maintains fertility) and personal hygiene are important for healthy sex organs. A number of diseases (such as HIV, AIDS, gonorrhoea, herpes, non specific urethritis [NSU – inflammation of the urethra]) can be transmitted sexually, though protection through condoms restricts this transfer. However, the safest and healthiest option is to maintain long standing and loving relationships where the partners are clear of disease. These are also the best conditions for emotional health and for the upbringing of children.

Attitudes in society to sex are very contradictory, however, with sexual messages and stimuli bombarding people from a wide range of sources. It is certainly worth holding discussions on the exploitive aspects of sex as expressed through tabloid and advertising images, for example, as these influences are pervasive and have wide ranging influences.

In teaching about reproduction and growth children need to understand the biological details, but there are a number of social and emotional issues which should be addressed within the context of the school's policy for sex education as determined by the governing body. The NCC document, *Curriculum Guidance: 5 Health Education* (1990b) recommends that pupils at Key Stage 2 should begin to know about and have some understanding of the physical, emotional and social changes which take place at puberty. They should have an understanding of the basic biology of human reproduction and understand some of the skills necessary for parenthood. The following will also need to be considered when covering this topic:

- HIV and Aids;
- child abuse;
- religious belief and sex education;
- special needs children in an integrated class.

The level of detail is best provided by questions which the children themselves provide. In the early stages of discussion questions written anonymously can help to avoid any initial embarrassment for children. As the discussion becomes relaxed the children will begin to ask the questions more openly.

Some useful checkpoints when teaching sex education in the primary school are:

- If you are likely to need help, ask for it.
- Don't be afraid to admit you don't know the answer.
- Facilitate discussion, but in a manner that is comfortable for you and therefore, for the pupils.
- Maintain the confidence of the pupils at all times.
- Respect confidentiality.

Family life education is another aspect of this topic. The NCC health education guidance (1990b) says that this involves relationships, child care and effective parenting. Pupils should develop an understanding of what is meant by relationships within families and that loving caring stable families come in a variety of forms. Child development from birth to five plus needs to be explored emphasising different patterns of child-rearing and the importance of 'good parenting'. Examples from a range of communities and cultures can be given.

The needs of the old and ill should be also discussed and pupils made aware of what happens at death. This section should highlight community, family and individual help agencies which are available offering counselling and guidance in a variety of circumstances.

Health and pathogens

Many people confuse viral infections with bacterial infections. A virus cannot make copies of itself without the help of the cell it invades. It is little more than some DNA which takes over the cell mechanism to make copies of itself. As it does so we get ill. We protect ourselves from viral infections (such as chicken pox) by catching the disease and making antibodies in our blood. When we next get an invasion of the virus, our blood is ready to respond. Inoculations (jabs), which contain a weakened form of the virus, do the same thing, but we get a very mild form of the disease which we hardly notice.

Bacteria (one bacterium) are fully independent single celled organisms, though still very small. Bacterial infections, such as tonsillitis, are treated with antibiotics. Bacteria can become resistant so it is important to use antibiotics carefully and always to finish the course you are given. Some diseases are caused by larger parasitic organisms, as in schistosomiasis (Bilharzia) or tapeworms.

Children need to understand and accept responsibility for personal clean-
liness, e.g. they should be encouraged to wash their hands after visiting the
toilet. The school should ensure that toilets are kept clean and that soap and
towels or functioning air driers are always available. Recognition should be given
to different cultural practices in personal hygiene and food handling.

Dental decay and good dental hygiene can be explored in relation to diet and
its possible detrimental affects on the body. At Key Stage 2 pupils will cover
changes at puberty and they need to be aware of how these changes affect the
body in relation to hygiene.

Inherited disorders

It is remarkable how reliable the growth process is – serious problems will
prevent a baby going to term. However, we are all different, and our genetic
make-up causes some of us to be more prone to some diseases than others.
Tendency to be asthmatic (and the related hay fever and eczema) is inherited.
The fact that some smokers don't get smoking-related diseases is probably due to
their genetic make up. One day we may be able to tell, through genetic testing, if
we are susceptible or not.

Safety

This is another important dimension of health education. Accidents are the most
common cause of death and disability in children: in a class of 30 children, on
average, every child will have to receive hospital treatment for two accidental
injuries before their 16th birthday and two will be killed or suffer serious injury on
the roads (ROSPA 1996). Children need to be taught how to be safe, to be aware
of hazards and to know how to prevent accidents. They need to know what to do
if an accident does happen and understand the language of safety. Role play and
drama are both effective vehicles through which to deliver such messages.

Case study 5: Year 5 drama project on health and our bodies

Two parallel year 5 classes followed a similar programme of classroom activities
to develop understanding of the body and related issues of health. In addition
one group experienced drama activities designed to make the children's concepts
and attitudes related to health and the body explicit. The activities were
negotiated with the children and are shown in Table 9.6. The medium was a TV
show (video recorded) with the ostensible aim of making a show which would
teach other children about health. The actual aim was to help the children who
were involved in making it clarify and share their ideas so that the concepts
developed in the class-based activities could be placed in an interesting,
meaningful and enjoyable context.

Stages of the drama	Activities
● brainstorming and selection of ideas	● discussion about interesting drama ideas for presenting a TV programme about health ● children select the ideas for sections of 'The Body Show' and choose their roles
● 'The Body Show': introduction	● presenters introduce the show which is intended to teach the audience (children of similar age) how to keep healthy and what not to do
● interviews to show what people may do which is healthy or unhealthy	● people leaving a supermarket are interviewed to find out what they have bought (showing healthy/unhealthy eating patterns) ● people are interviewed; in a street, park, outside a leisure centre to find out about exercise patterns
● studio guests, the *Crock* family are interviewed by the main presenters (and demonstrate very unhealthy patterns)	● *Glut* overeats and suffers from obesity ● *Annie Rexia* diets excessively ● *Grease* eats too many fatty foods ● *Sweet-tooth* eats too many sugary foods ● *Slob* takes no exercise at all ● *Smog* smokes excessively
● a new presenter enters and introduces a new part to the show 'This is your body' (like the TV programme 'This is your life') The Crocks are shown what is happening to their bodies as a result of their particular life style	● each *Crock* family member is taken on a conducted tour of their body by the *Body Explorers* who are made microscopically small by a 'micro time travelling machine', enter the body and describe the conditions inside ● after this they are transported into the future and describe what it is like after many years have passed ● they describe excess fat in *Glut* who has a heart attack from high blood pressure. *Slob* is very unfit, has a weak heart and suffers a similar fate. *Annie Rexia* is too thin and becomes very ill and weak. ● the *Sugar Finders* describe *Sweet-tooth's* mouth with decaying teeth which eventually fall out ● the *Fat Detectives* show that *Grease* has occluded arteries and eventually has a heart attack ● the *Lung Men* describe *Smog's* lungs which eventually develop a cancer tumour
● audience 'phone in'	● to give advice to the *Crocks* about how they may become more healthy
● problems of temptation (to illustrate the problems of peer pressure)	● scenes to show how it is not always easy to make healthy choices (the action is 'frozen' at a crucial point and 'spoken thoughts' give the thoughts and dilemmas of the person being tempted) ● a group of secondary students are smoking and offer one to a friend who isn't ● another group offers drugs to a friend ● a group of children in a shop choose very unhealthy foods - what does their friend choose?
● audience phone in to a panel of experts	● a doctor, dentist/hygienist and psychiatrist answer questions about difficulties in making choices (groups of children discuss the possible answers before the character in role speaks)
● the *Crocks* are re-interviewed	● they describe how they have taken the previous advice to improve their health and how their bodies have improved
● finale ● editing and completion	● the presenter summarises what makes healthy living ● the show finishes with a 'health rap' created by the children ● the video material is edited and the completed 'Body Show' is made

Table 9.6 Stages of the drama in a Year 5 project on health and our bodies

The 'Health Rap' associated with the drama shows how learning in science can be fun, with a personal message for action for health:

The Health Rap (devised by a previous y6 group involved with a similar project – see Littledyke, 1994c):

If you wanna stay healthy if you wanna stay cool,
You've gotta remember these golden rules,
Be careful what you eat,
Be careful what you do,
If you don't look out you've got it coming to you.
It's a rap,
It's the healthy rap.

If you wanna be a sugar freak or eat lots of fat,
You're gonna die of a heart attack.
If you pay no attention to what you've just seen,
You'll never ever ever learn what we mean.
You'll fall flat
From a heart attack.

If you wanna flash you're teeth, if you wanna look good,
You'd better cut down on the sugary food.
Eat less biscuits and cakes and sweets
Or your teeth will ache and ache for weeks.
They'll go black,
Then they'll all fall out.

Don't smoke fags it don't look big,
You'll only end up sick as a pig.
Nicotine and tar that's in the smoke,
They'll give you cancer and that's no joke.
You'll be dead,
So don't be soft in the head.

If you wanna keep slim then go to the gym.
'Oh no, oh no, not the gym.' (Smogs' chorus)
If you wanna stay hip, if you wanna stay dude
You've got to eat all the helathy foods,
And stay clean.
Don't you know what we mean.

So we hope you've listened to what we've said,
You wanna stay well not drop down dead.
It makes good sense to keep fit and cool,
So you'd better remember the golden rules
Of the rap,
The healthy rap.

This teaching programme was part of a research project funded by the Teacher Training Agency (Littledyke *et al.* 1997c): see also Chapter 3 for another part of the project and Littledyke (1994c) for similar project involving drama and health. Interviews and assessment of children's understanding of the important scientific concepts associated with health and the body showed that the children who had experienced the drama activities had statistically significantly better conceptual understanding than the control group which did not experience the drama. They were also able to articulate and reason their views better and showed higher levels of interest and motivation: they said they 'had a great time' on the project and 'learnt lots about the body and health' in the process; ideas which will hopefully prepare them for healthy lifestyle choices as they grow into independent adults.

References

Appleyard, B. (1992) *Understanding the Present: Science and the Soul of Modern Man.* London: Pan.

Ausubel, D. (1968) *Educational Psychology.* NY: Holt Rinehart and Winston.

Axelrod, R. (1984) *The Evolution of Cooperation.* New York: Basic Books.

Barnes, D. (1976) *From Communication to Curriculum.* London: Penguin Educational.

BBC 2 (1992) *Prisoners of the Sun.* Bristol: BBC TV.

Bernstein, M., Sandford, S. and Allamandola, L. (1999) *Life's Far-Flung Raw Materials.* http://www.sciam.com/1999/0799issue0799bernstein.html

Birch, C. (1988) 'The Postmodern Challenge to Biology', in Griffin, D. R. (ed.), *The Reenchantment of Science: Postmodern Proposals.* Albany: State University of New York Press.

Bohm, D. (1983) *Wholeness and the Implicate Order.* London: Ark.

Borgford, A. (1992) *Change in Science Teaching and Science Content.* York: University of Science Education Group.

Bourne, P. D. (1971) 'From Boot Camp to My Lai', in Falk, R. Kolko, G. and Lifton, R. (eds), *Crimes of War.* New York: Random House.

Brickhouse, N. (1991) 'Teachers' content knowledge about the nature of science and its relationship to classroom practice', *Journal of Teacher Education* **41**, 53–62.

Briggs, J. (1992) *Fractals: The patterns of chaos.* London: Thames and Hudson.

Brook, A. Driver, R. and Johnston, K. (1989) in Wellington, J. (ed) *Skills and Processes in Science Education. A classroom perspective.* London: Routledge.

Browne, B. (1997) in Edwards, A. and Knight, P. *Effective Early Years Education.* Buckingham: Open University Press.

Bruner, J. S. (1966) *Studies in Cognitive Growth.* New York: Wiley.

Butt. N. (1991) *Science and Muslim Societies.* London: Grey Seal Books.

Capra, F. (1975) *The Tao of Physics.* Berkeley: Shambala.

Capra, F. (1982) *The Turning Point.* London: Fontana.

Carson, R. (1962) *Silent Spring.* Harmondsworth: Penguin.

CASE (1999) http://www.wdu.dudley.gov.uk/saltwells/science/case2.html

Channel 4 (1993) *Simple Minds.* London: Channel 4 TV.

Charlton, T. and David, K. (1989) *Managing Misbehaviour: Strategies for Effective Management of Behaviour in Schools.* London: Macmillan Education.

Clayden, E., Desforges, C., Mills, C. and Rawson, W. (1994) 'Authentic activity and learning', *British Journal of Educational Studies* **60**, 163–73.

Cobb, J. Jr. (1988) 'Ecology, Science and Religion: Toward a Postmodern View', in Griffin, D. R. (ed.) *The Reenchantment of Science: Postmodern Proposals.* Albany: State University of New York Press.

Concar, D. and Coghlan, A. (1999) 'A question of breeding', *New Scientist*, February, 4–5.

Conner, S. (1997) 'The Fruit and Nut Case', G2 *The Guardian Newpaper*, 3 June.

Davies, P. (1983) *God and the New Physics.* London: J. M. Dent and Sons.

Dawkins, R. (1989) *The Selfish Gene.* Oxford: Oxford University Press.

Dennett, D. C. (1993) *Consciousness Explained.* London: Viking.

Department for Education (DfE) (1995) *Key Stages 1 and 2 of the National Curriculum.* London: HMSO.

Department for Education and Employment (DfEE) (1998) *Initial teacher training National Curriculum for Primary Science (Annex E of Circular 4/98).* London: HMSO.

Department of the Environment (DoE) (1995) *Climate Change.* Issue 4. London: HMSO.

Department for Trade and Industry (DTI) (1998) 'UK Energy in Brief', *Department of Trade and Industry.* London: HMSO.

Diamond, J. (1992) *The Rise and Fall of the Third Chimpanzee: how our animal heritage affects the way we live.* London: Vintage.

Drengson, A.R. (1989) *Beyond Environmental Crisis: From Technocratic to Planetary Person.* New York: Peter Lang.

Driver, R. (1975) 'The name of the game', *School Science Review* **56**(197), 800–5.

Driver, R. (1985) 'Pupils' alternative frameworks in science', in Hodgson, B. and Scanlon, E. (eds) *Approaching Primary Science.* London: Harper and Row.

Driver R. and Bell, B. (1986) 'Students' thinking and the learning of science: a constructivist view', *School Science Review* **67**, 443–56.

Driver, R., Guesne T. and Tiberghien, A. (1985) *Children's Ideas in Science.* Milton Keynes, Open University.

Driver, R., Squires, A., Rushworth, P. and Wood-Robinson, V. (1994) *Making Sense of Secondary Science.* London: Routledge.

Duschl, R. and Wright, E. (1989) 'A case study of high school teachers' decision making models for planning and teaching science', *Journal of Research in Science Teaching* **26**, 467–502.

Eagan, D. J. and Orr, D. W. (eds) (1992) *The Campus and Environmental Responsibility.* San Francisco: Jossey-Bass.

Eder, K. (1996) *The Social Construction of Nature.* London: Sage.

Edmondson, K. and Novak, J. (1993) 'The interplay of scientific epistemological views, learning strategies and attitudes of college students', *Journal of Research in Science Teaching* **30**(6), 547–59.

Einstein, A. (1923) *Sidelights on Relativity.* New York: E. P. Dutton.

Elliott, D. (1997) *Energy, Society and Environment.* London: Routledge.

Ferre, F. (1988) 'Religious World Modelling and Postmodern Science', in Griffin, D. R. (ed.) *The Reenchantment of Science: Postmodern Proposals.* Albany: State University of New York Press.

Fien, J. (1995) 'Teaching for a Sustainable World: the Environment and Development Education Project for Teacher Education', *Environmental Education Research* **1**(1), 21–33.

Fox, W. (1990) *Toward a Transpersonal Ecology.* Massachusetts: Shambala.

Foucault, M. (1977) *Discipline and Punish: The Birth of Prison.* Harmondsworth: Penguin.

Gayford, C. G. and Dillon, P. J. (1995) 'Policy and Practice of Environmental Education in England: a dilemma for teachers', *Environmental Education Research* **1**(2), 173–83.

Glance, N. S. and Huberman, B. A. (1994) 'The Dynamics of Social Dilemmas', *Scientific American*, March, 58–63.

Gleick, J. (1988) *Chaos: Making a New Science.* London: Heinemann.

Goldsmith, E. *et al.* (1972) 'A blueprint for survival', The Ecologist **2**(1), 1–43.

Gough, N. (1990) 'Healing the Earth Within Us: Environmental Education as Cultural Criticism', *The Journal of Experiential Education*, **13**(3), 12–7.

Gould, S. J. (1990) *Wonderful Life: The Burgess Shale and the Nature of History.* London: Hutchinson Radius.

Griffin, D. R. (ed.) (1988) *The Reenchantment of Science: Postmodern Proposals.* Albany: State University of New York Press.

Harlen, W. (1985) *Primary Science – Taking the Plunge.* Oxford: Heinemann Education.

Harlen, W. (1992) *The Teaching of Science.* London: David Fulton.

Harvey, D. (1989) *The Condition of Postmodernity.* Oxford: Blackwell.

Harvey, J. and Passmore, S. (1995) 'School Nutrition Action Groups', *The Home Economist* **14**(3), 13–14.

Hawking, S.H. (1988) *A Brief History of Time: from the big bang to black holes.* London: Bantam.

Hertiage, J. (1999) 'There is no such thing as safe food', *Biologist* **46**(3), 100.

Holdich, D. (1994) 'The British crayfish – a threatened species', *Biological Science Review* **6**(5), 12–3.

Holmes, B. (1997) 'When we were Worms', *New Scientist,* October, 30–5.

Howard, S. (1998) 'A Future for the Forest' *Biological Science Review* **10**(3), 25–30.

Humphrey, N. (1993) *The Inner Eye.* Vintage: London.

Intergovernmental Panel on Climate Change (IPCC) (1992), *Second Assessment of Scientific-Technical Information Relevant to Interpreting Article 2 of the UN Framework Convention on Climate Change.* London: HMSO.

Jeffries, M. (1997) *Biodiversity and Conservation.* London: Routledge.

Jiménez, M. P., Gayoso, A. and Gayoso, I. G. (1996) 'An Approach to Introducing Environmental Education into the Science Methods Course in Teacher Education', *Environmental Education Research* **2**(1), 27–39.

Johnstone, J. (1998) 'Learning Science in the Early Years', in Sherrington, R. (ed.) *ASE Guide to Primary Science Education.* Hatfield: ASE.

Jones, C. (1997) 'Ecosystems', *Biological Science Review* **9**(4), 9–14.

Kirkham, J. (1989) 'Skills and Processes in Science Education', in Wellington, J. (ed.) *Balanced Science: equilibrium between context, processes and content.* London: Routledge.

Kohlberg, L. (1976) 'Moral Stages and Moralisation: The Cognitive Developmental Approach', in Likona, T. (ed.) *Moral Development and Behaviour: Theory, Research and Social Issues.* New York: Holt, Reinhart and Winston.

Kuhn, T. (1970) *The Structure of Scientific Revolutions.* Chicago: University of Chicago Press.

LaChapelle, D. (1991) 'Educating for Deep Ecology', *The Journal of Experiential Education* **14**(3), 18–22.

Lakin, S. and Wellington, J. (1994) 'Who will teach the "nature of science"?: teachers' views of science and their implications for science education', *International Journal of Science Education* **16**, 175–90.

Lantz, O. And Kass, H. (1987) 'Chemistry teachers' functional paradigms', *Science Education* **71**, 117–34.

Leopold, A. (1949) *A Sand County Almanac: And Sketches Here and There.* Oxford: Oxford University Press.

Levitt, M. (1999) 'Genes à la Carte', *Biologist* **46**(3), 105–8.

Littledyke, M. (1989) 'Employment Versus Pollution', *Questions,* November, 21–24.

Littledyke, M. (1994a) 'Primary Teacher Responses to the National Curriculum for Science', *School Science Review* **75**, 106–16.

Littledyke, M. (1994b) 'Employment Versus Environment', 'The People That Time Forgot', in *Projects for Science and Technology with Drama.* London: Watts and Questions Publishing Company.

Littledyke, M. (1994c) 'The Health Show', *Questions* **7**(2), Nov/Dec.

Littledyke, M. (1996) 'Science Education for Environmental Awareness in a Postmodern World', *Environmental Education Research* **2**(2), 197–214.

Littledyke, M. (1997a) 'Science education for environmental education? Primary teacher perspectives and practices', *British Educational Research Journal* **23**(5), 641–59.

Littledyke, M. (1997b) 'Science Education for Environmental Awareness', *Publication of the 3rd summer conference for teacher education in primary science.* Durham University.

Littledyke, M. (1998) *Live Issues: Drama Strategies for Personal, Social and Moral Education.* Birmingham: Questions.

Littledyke, M. and Huxford, L. (eds) (1998) *Teaching the Primary Curriculum for Constructive Learning.* London: David Fulton.

Littledyke, M., Oldroyd, J. and Robertson, J. (1997) 'The Impact of Primary Science Teaching on Children's Attitudes to and Understanding of Health and Environmental Issues', Teacher Training Agency Research Project. Cheltenham: Cheltenham and Gloucester College of Higher Education.

Littledyke, M., Ross, K., Sutton, D., Lakin, L. and Shepherd, J. (1999) *Teaching Primary Science: Course guide and study book*. Cheltenham: Cheltenham and Gloucester College of Higher Education.

Losee, J. (1993) *A Historical Introduction to the Philosophy of Science*. 3rd edn. Oxford: Oxford University Press.

Lyon, D. (1994) *Postmodernity*. Buckingham: Open University Press.

MacMillain, W. (1996) 'What's ahead for a global food industry', *The Home Economist* **15**(4).

Maslow, A. H. (1968) *Towards a Psychology of Being*, 2nd edn. New York: Harper and Row.

Matthews, M. (1994) *Science Teaching: The Role of History and Philosophy of Science*. London: Routledge.

Maybury-Lewis, D. (1991) *Millennium: Tribal Wisdom of the Modern World*. London: Viking.

McKibbon, B. (1990) *The End of Nature*. London: Penguin.

Medawar, P. (1979) 'Is the Scientific Paper a Fraud?', London: BBC Publications, reprinted in Brown, J., Cooper, A., Horton, T., Toates, F. and Zeldin, D. (eds) *Science in Schools*, 43–47. Milton Keynes: Open University Press.

Merchant, C. (1980) *The Death of Nature: Women, Ecology and the Scientific Revolution*. New York: Harper and Row.

Milgram, S. (1974) *Obedience to Authority*. London: Tavistock.

Millar, R. (1991) 'A Means to an End: the role of processes in science education', in Woolnough, B. (ed.) *Practical Science*. Milton Keynes: Open University Press.

Millar, R. (1994) 'What is scientific method and can it be taught?' in Levingson, R. (ed.) *Teaching Science*. London: Routledge.

Millar, R. and Osborne, J. (1998) *Beyond 2000 Science Education for the future*. London: King's College London.

Meadows, D. H., Meadows, D. L., Randers, J. and Behrens, W. (1972) *The Limits to Growth: A Report for the Club of Rome's Project on the Predicament of mankind*. London: Pan.

Monod, J. (1972) *Chance and Necessity*. London: Collins.

Morris, S. (1992) 'Beginnings: A Journey to the Dawn of Animal Life', *Biological Science Review* **4**(4), 31–5.

Naess, A. (1973) 'The shallow and the deep long-range ecology movements', *Inquiry* **16**, 95–100.

Naess, A. (1989) *Ecology, Community and Lifestyle: Outline of an Ecosophy*. Translated and revised by Rothenberg, D., Cambridge: Cambridge University Press.

National Curriculum Council (1990a) *Curriculum Guidance 7: Environmental Education*. York: NCC.

National Curriculum Council (1990b) *Curriculum Guidance 5: Health Education*. York: NCC.

National Farmers Union (NFU) (1997) 'Farming Today', Radio 4 broadcast.

Nuffield Primary Science Science Processes and Concept Exploration (SPACE) (1995) *Living Processes*. London: Collins.

Ollerenshaw, C. and Ritchie, R. (1993) *Primary Science: making it work*. London: David Fulton.

Osborne, R. and Freyberg, P. (1985) *Learning in Science: The implications of Children's Science*. Auckland: Heinemann.

Papadimitriou, V. (1996) 'Environmental Education within a Science Course in the Initial Education of Primary Teachers', *Environmental Education Research* **2**(1), 17–26.

Parker, A. (1999) 'The Cambrian Explosion', *Biologist* **46**(1), 26–30.

Pattinson, J. (1998) 'Exposing the Wobbly Bits', *Primary Science Review* **53**(25), May/June, p. 25.

Peace Child International (1994) 'Rescue Mission Planet Earth', *A Children's Edition of Agenda 21*. London: Kingfisher.

Pecujac, I. (1998) *Images of Health*, Bendigo, Australia: Video Education Australia.

Pennington, H. (1999) 'Lessons from GM Potatoes', *Biologist* **46**(2), p. 51.

Pinker, S. (1998) *How the Mind Works*. London: Penguin.

Polkinghorne Committee (1993) *Report of the Committee on the Ethics of Genetic Modification and Food Use*. London: HMSO.

Polkinghorne, J. (1999) 'Science and Religion in the 21st Century', Publication of conference paper on science and religion. London: Hinde Methodist Church.

Popper, K. (1963) *Conjectures and Refutations*. London: Routledge, Keegan and Paul.

Poundstone, W. (1992) *Prisoner's Dilemma*. Oxford: Oxford University Press.

PRECIS 6 (1987) *The Culture of Fragments*. New York: Columbia University Graduate School of Architecture, pp. 7–24.

Qualter, A. (1996) *Differentiated Primary Science*. London: Oxford University Press.

Reiss, M. (1993) 'Developing Science and Technology Education', in *Science Education for a Pluralist Society*. Buckingham: Oxford University Press.

Rorty, R. (1982) *Consequences of Pragmatism*. Minneapolis: University of Minnesota Press.

Ross, K.A. (1989) A Cross-cultural Study of People's Understanding of the Functioning of Fuels and the Process of Burning. Unpublished PhD Thesis, University of Bristol.

Ross, K. A. (1991) 'Burning: a constructive not a destructive process', in *School Science Review* **72**(251) 45–49.

Ross, K. A. (1997) 'Many substances but only five structures', *School Science Review* **78**(284) 79–87.

Ross, K. (1998) 'Brenda grapples with the properties of a mern', in Littledyke, M. and Huxford, L. (eds) *Teaching the Primary Curriculum for Constructive Learning*. London: David Fulton.

Ross, K. A. and Lakin, E. (1996) *The Science of Environmental Issues*. Cheltenham: The Cheltenham and Gloucester College of Higher Education.

Ross, K. A. and Lakin, E. (1998) *The Science of Environmental Issues*. CDROM: Cheltenham: The Cheltenham and Gloucester College of Higher Education.

Roszak, T. (1970) *The Making of a Counter Culture*. London: Faber and Faber.

Royal Society for the Prevention of Accidents (1996) 'Together Safely', *Safety Education*, Summer, Birmingham: ROSPA

Sagan, C. and Druyan, A. (1993) *Shadows of Forgotten Ancestors*. London: Arrow.

Schumacher, E. F. (1973) *Small is Beautiful*. London: Abacus.

Scottish Health Education Group and the World Health Organisation (1989) 'The Healthy School', *Safety Education*, Summer, Birmingham: ROSPA

Sessions, G. (1974) 'Anthropocentrism and the Environmental Crisis', *Humboldt Journal of Social Relations*, **2**, 71–81.

Solomon, J., Duveen, J. and Scott, L. (1994) 'Pupils' images of scientific epistemology', *International Journal of Science Education* **16**(3), 361–73.

Smith, M. J. (1998) *Ecologism: Towards Ecological Citizenship*. Buckingham: Open University Press.

SPACE (Science Processes And Concept Exploration) Project (various reports 1989–92) *Research reports into children's understanding in Growth, Light, Forces, Sound, Electricity Materials*. Liverpool: University of Liverpool Press.

Stannard, R. (1995) *Our Universe*. London: Kingfisher.

Stockley, P. (1999) 'An RNA World', *Biological Science Review* **11**(3), 2–6.

Sutton, C.R. (1992) *Words, Science and Learning*. Buckingham: Open University Press.

Swimme, B (1988) 'The Cosmic Creation Story', in Griffin, D. R. (ed.), *The Reenchantment of Science: Postmodern Proposals*. Albany: State University of New York Press.

The Independent (1999) 'The Eclipse', *The Independent*, Thursday 12 August.

Thomas, K. (1982) *Man and the Natural World 1500–1800*. Harmondsworth: Penguin.

Thoreau, H. D. (1886) in Dircks, W. H. (ed.) *Walden, or Life in the Woods*, London: Walter Scott Publishing.

Trotman, C. (1998) 'Origins of Life', *Biologist* **45**(2), 76–80.

Waldrop, M. M. (1994) *Complexity: The Emerging Science at the Edge of Order and Chaos*. London: Penguin.

Weber, R. (1990) *Dialogues with Scientists and Sages*. London: Arkana.

West, R. (ed.) (1984) *Towards the Specification of Minimum Entitlement: Brenda and Friends*. London: Schools Council Publications.

White, L. (1967) 'The historical roots of our ecological crisis', *Science*, **155**, 1203–7.

Wittgenstein, L. (1951) *Tractatus Logico-Philosophicus*. London: Routledge Keegan and Paul.

Wolpert, L. (1992) *The Unnatural Nature of Science*. London: Faber.

Woolnough, B (ed.) (1991) *Practical Science*. Milton Keynes: Open University Press.

Ziman, J. (1968) *Public Knowledge*. Cambridge: Cambridge University Press.

Index